Identity Theft Devotional Study Guide

Identity Theft

Devotional Study Guide

By Laurie Dodds

Bold Vision Books
P.O. Box 2011
Friendswood, Texas 77549

©Copyright 2013 Laurie Dodds

Printed in the U.S.A.

Bold Vision Books
P.O. Box 2011
Friendswood, Texas 77549
www.boldvisionbooks.com

Book Development by Karen Porter, www.kaecreativesolutions.com
Cover by John Magee, John Magee Design, www.johnmageedesign.com

Scripture quotations marked NIV are taken from the Holy Bible, New International Version®, NIV®. Copyright © 1973, 1978, 1984, 2011 by Biblica, Inc.™ Used by permission of Zondervan. All rights reserved worldwide. www.zondervan.com The "NIV" and "New International Version" are trademarks registered in the United States Patent and Trademark Office by Biblica, Inc.™

Scripture quotations marked NKJV are taken from the New King James Version®. Copyright © 1982 by Thomas Nelson, Inc. Used by permission. All rights reserved.

Scripture quotations marked AMP are taken from the Amplified Bible Copyright © 1960, 1962, 1963, 1968, 1971, 1972, 1973, 1975, 1977, 1995 by The Lockman Foundation. Used by permission. (www.Lockman.org).

Scripture quotations marked NASB are taken from the New American Standard Bible®, Copyright © 1960, 1962, 1963, 1968, 1971, 1972, 1973, 1975, 1977, 1995 by The Lockman Foundation. Used by permission. (www.Lockman.org).

Scripture quotations marked GW are taken from GOD'S WORD®. Copyright 1995 God's Word to the Nations. Used by permission of Baker Publishing Group. All rights reserved.

Scripture quotations marked ESV are taken from The Holy Bible, English Standard Version® (ESV®) Copyright © 2001 by Crossway, a publishing ministry of Good News Publishers. All rights reserved. ESV Text Edition: 2007.

Scripture quotations marked RSV or NRSV are taken from the Revised Standard Version of the Bible, Copyright © 1952 [2nd edition, 1971] by the Division of Christian Education of the National Council of the Churches of Christ in the United States of America. Used by permission. All rights reserved.

Scripture quotations marked KJV are taken from the Holy Bible, King James Version, Cambridge, 1769.

Scripture quotations marked The Message are taken from The Message, Copyright© by Eugene H. Peterson 1993, 1994, 1995, 1996, 2000, 2001, 2002. Used by permission of NavPress Publishing Group.

Scripture quotations marked NLT are taken from the Holy Bible, New Living Translation, copyright © 1996, 2004, 2007 by Tyndale House Foundation. Used by permission of Tyndale House Publishers, Inc., Carol Stream, Illinois 60188. All rights reserved.

Scripture quotations marked TLB are taken from The Living Bible copyright © 1971. Used by permission of Tyndale House Publishers, Inc., Carol Stream, Illinois 60188. All rights reserved.

TABLE OF CONTENTS

Week One – My Identity
Day One	Identity's Source
Day Two	Identity's Perception
Day Three	Identity's Creator
Day Four	Identity's Purpose
Day Five	Identity's Role

Week Two – God Approves of You
Day One	Value
Day Two	Worth
Day Three	Choice
Day Four	Praise
Day Five	Loved

Week Three – Characteristics of Your God-given Identity
Day One	Redeemed
Day Two	Righteous
Day Three	Restored
Day Four	Responsive
Day Five	Re-focused

Week Four – Strategies of the Thief
Day One	He Robs
Day Two	He Lies
Day Three	He Misrepresents
Day Four	He Accuses
Day Five	He Seduces

Week Five – Defeat the Thief
Day One	Chosen and Accepted
Day Two	Full Life
Day Three	Never Alone
Day Four	Called
Day Five	Beneficiary

Week Six – Identity's Guard is the Holy Spirit
Day One   God's CPR
Day Two   Conviction
Day Three   Transformation
Day Four   Protection
Day Five   Freedom

Week Seven – Flourish in your True Identity
Day One   Potential
Day Two   Supernatural
Day Three   Love
Day Four   Legacy
Day Five   Reestablished

Welcome to **Identity Theft – Devotional Study Guide**.

It is my desire to walk with you as we discover true identity in Christ. For many years I've had the privilege of teaching beautiful, interesting, and remarkable women. These women come in different packages—various ages and sizes, assorted faiths and denominations, and diverse social and economic backgrounds. Many of these women wouldn't consider themselves attractive or appealing, but God sees each one as lovely and extraordinary. Our differences make us unique, yet I have discovered one glaring similarity: We have questions.

Who am I? Why am I here? Do I have a purpose? Do I have a divine purpose? Can I make a difference in my world? What is my value and worth?

God has the answers to all of these questions. God invites us to find our true identity. When we discover how we are "wonderfully made,"[i] we will understand how unique and irreplaceable we are. God is our Creator and He built into each one of us a purpose and a plan. His plan is far greater than we could ever hope, dream, or imagine.

After talking with women who have read my book or heard me speak about "Identity Theft," I came to an even greater understanding of the importance of grasping our true identity. I wanted to give you another resource to help you define your identity and learn to live in the strength and confidence God intended. Use the next seven weeks as a time of study and devotional to discover and absorb your true identity. At the end of each week, look for the section *Going Deeper*. Use this resource to reflect, ponder, and memorize.

I'm looking forward to spending these weeks with you, and I can hardly wait until you discover and recognize the beautiful woman God made you to be. I would love to hear your identity story. Connect with me at dodds.laurie@gmail.com.

Laurie Dodds

Week One – My Identity

Welcome to Week One. This week we will look at the underpinnings of identity. We will focus on the foundation and the Father of our unique identity. We will do the hard work of determining how we view our own identity compared with how God sees us, and by the end of the week, we will have a new perspective and perhaps even a new dream.

God's primary concern is not about what I do. This statement may surprise you, but think about it deeply. God's love is not performance-based. Oh, sure, He expects us to live in the fullness of His gifts—love, joy, peace, strength, and power—but His greatest desires for us have to do with who we are becoming not what we have been doing. He wants us to mature and be strong. He wants our private life and our public persona to be the same. Instead of pretending to be strong believers, He wants us to really believe.

Paul explained this deeper identity to the Ephesian church:

> I pray that from his glorious, unlimited resources he will empower you with inner strength through his Spirit. Then Christ will make his home in your hearts as you trust in him. Your roots will grow down into God's love and keep you strong. And may you have the power to understand, as all God's people should, how wide, how long, how high, and how deep his love is. May you experience the love of Christ, though it is too great to understand fully. Then you will be made complete with all the fullness of life and power that comes from God (Ephesians 3:16–19 NLT).

We will study these verses in depth in week two. In the meantime, I am praying this verse over myself and over you as you embark on the journey to greater understanding of your identity. May you be made complete in Him.

This week we will discover the source of our identity — our Creator God. We will also encounter the source and role identity plays in our life and spiritual growth. Let's get started.

Week One
Day One
Identity's Source

I heard a story of a man traveling through Hong Kong. As he passed by a tattoo shop, he noticed a design in the window, "Born to Lose." Astonished at the idea that anyone would want to affix those words to their body permanently, he stepped into the shop.

"Has anyone ever actually bought that tattoo?" he asked.

The elderly tattoo artist responded, "Yes. First tattoo in the mind, then tattoo on the body."[ii]

Powerful words. First in the mind, then on the body.

I have a friend who read a bumper sticker, "Hated by All." She wondered how the person driving the car must feel to put such a bumper sticker on his or her car.

When it comes to identity, how we think affects how we live. We may not have a tattoo or a bumper sticker, but our traits are etched into the membranes of our hearts and souls. Every thought, action, reaction, and comment reflects what we believe about ourselves.

Read Proverbs 23:7:

> For as [a man] thinketh in his heart, so is he (KJV).

The way we think reveals how we feel about ourselves.

Knowing our true identity is vital. What words or ideas are tattooed in your mind? Think about it. In the space below write a few (at least three) descriptive words about your identity.

_____
_____
_____
_____

How did you define yourself? What thoughts came to your mind? What if I told you that God describes you as chosen, special, forgiven, accepted, and loved? These are love words of God toward you. Carefully consider these words. Read God's list again. One at a time.

>You are chosen.
>You are special.
>You are forgiven.
>You are accepted.
>You are loved.

How does the list compare with the way you see yourself? Did you choose any of those words? If you are like most people, you didn't use God's words to describe yourself. Unfortunately, His words are usually not the ones tattooed on our minds.

You probably chose words to describe your accomplishments, words others have spoken about you, or words that describe how you feel about yourself.

Often we try to derive our identity from

- what we've done or haven't done,
- what we've achieved or haven't achieved,
- what others think or don't think of us,
- what others have said or not said about us, or
- how we feel or don't feel.

Opinions are subjective. Emotions waver. Impressions fluctuate. Judgments can be faulty. If we try to get our identity from a perfect performance or people's opinions, we will be apprehensive and uncomfortable throughout life. If flawlessness is our goal, we will be anxious, unsettled, and confused about who we are and why we are here on earth.

I had only been out of college a few years when I was asked to serve on the finance committee of our church. Even though I was a banking executive, the invitation to serve was humbling. At the first meeting, I felt nervous because there were only two women on the committee and everyone seemed much older and wiser. Can you say, "Over my head"? Throughout the meeting I participated to the best of my ability, yet there was an uncomfortable feeling and a definite lack of acceptance. Later, when my husband asked how it went, I told him how awkward the evening felt and how no one seemed to take me seriously. Disappointed and frustrated, I turned to leave the room only to hear Duncan's quiet laughter. He could barely contain himself. "Do you know you have two curlers in the back of your hair?"

I sat on the front row of the meeting with dozens of impressive businessmen all around me with curlers sticking in the back of my hair. *No wonder they did not take me seriously.*

Acceptance by others (or not-so-perfect hair) does not define me—unless I let it.

Which of the following should be the true source of your identity?

- ☐ Opinions of others
- ☐ Failure or accomplishment
- ☐ Possessions or physical attractiveness
- ☐ Applause
- ☐ Feelings
- ☐ None of the above

If our identity is based on the opinions of others, then we will become a slave to the fluctuating status of feelings. If our identity is based on failure or accomplishment, we only think we are worthy when we succeed. If our identity is defined by possessions or physical attractiveness, whether they are good or bad, we become discontented because outward factors are subject to change. If our identity is based on applause, we may compromise our values in order to obtain praise. If our identity is based on feelings, we waver with every emotion.

True identity is not grounded on these definitions. True identity has a different foundation. True identity reflects its source. We are not what we do or what others think we are. Our identity is established in the deep love of our Father God. His opinion is all that matters. He loves us no matter what we do or how we look or what we have. He loves us on stage and off, and His love transcends any emotion.

> See what great love the Father has lavished on us, that
> we should be called children of God! And that is what

> we are! The reason the world does not know us is that it did not know him. Dear friends, now we are children of God, and what we will be has not yet been made known. But we know that when Christ appears, we shall be like him, for we shall see him as he is. All who have this hope in him purify themselves, just as he is pure (1 John 3:1–3 NIV).

The Father's love is described as "lavish." It is a deep, abundant, generous, extravagant love. Understanding how much He loves us is a foundational truth vital to comprehending and appreciating our identity. The Father's love is the source of our identity.

Your life, if lived in true identity, will be authentic. You will be a genuine reflection of the Father. You will become a hope-giver who anticipates the best from God and draws others into the same optimism and confidence. Your true identity will spread joy to everyone you meet. He is your source and your strength. He is the beginning of true identity.

Week One
Day Two
Identity's Perception

Look back at your list of descriptive words from Day One.

With that list in mind, spend a few minutes answering the following questions.

Have you ever tried to figure out what some other person wanted you to be and then tried to be that person for them? Describe that situation here.

_____
_____
_____
_____
_____

A friend of mine described how she rose to the top of the corporate ranks by pretending to be the tough administrator she thought the male executives wanted her to be. She demanded perfection from her staff. She was unbending and hardheaded as she dealt with customers and employees. She developed an inflexible role as a manager. Stress and anxiety ruled her department. Yes, she rose through the ranks to the top of the corporate ladder, but when she got there, she was miserable, frustrated, and unfulfilled because she was living in a false identity, trying to be what she thought others wanted her to be.

What do you think others want you to be?

_____
_____

The last time you made a major decision did you seek the opinions and approval of others? Describe what happened.

_____
_____
_____
_____

Write about some advice you received that turned out to be more destructive than helpful.

_____
_____
_____
_____

When you make a decision, how do you decide?

      a. Based on how you feel
      b. Based on what someone might say
      c. Based on advice
      d. Based on your desires

If you perceive your identity from feelings, desires, approval, advice, and outward appearance, then you might make decisions founded on emotional responses.

What are some results of misplaced perception when making decisions?

_____
_____
_____

The only way to offset the effect of making poor decisions is to understand the way God sees us. If we are overtly worried about what others think, we can cave into criticism or live as if life is a performance, but what actually matters is God's opinion.

The prophet Samuel anointed Saul as king of Israel. Saul was a handsome man who stood head and shoulders taller than all the other men of the land. He looked like a king. However, Saul's perception of his own identity was low.

When the prophet told Saul he would be king, Saul responded with false identity.

> Saul replied, "But I'm only from the tribe of Benjamin, the smallest tribe in Israel, and my family is the least important of all the families of that tribe! Why are you talking like this to me?" (1 Samuel 9:21 NLT).

Saul felt he was too small, from the wrong side of the tracts, and just a Benjamite, from the smallest clan. A no name. He was unsure of himself and his God-given identity. Even after being anointed king by the great prophet, Saul was reticent. At his inaugural, he hid among the baggage.

> Then he brought each family of the tribe of Benjamin before the LORD, and the family of the Matrites was chosen. And finally Saul son of Kish was chosen from among them. But when they looked for him, he had disappeared! So they asked the LORD, "Where is he?"
>
> And the LORD replied, "He is hiding among the baggage." So they found him and brought him out, and he stood head and shoulders above anyone else.
>
> Then Samuel said to all the people, "This is the man the LORD has chosen as your king. No one in all Israel is like him!"
>
> And all the people shouted, "Long live the king!" (1 Samuel 10:21–24 NLT)

He was the king. He stood taller and more handsome than anyone else did. There was no one in all Israel like him, yet he hid like a bashful, frightened child. He allowed his fear to mask his true identity in God.

As you consider Saul's situation, ponder what God might have waiting for you if you will stop hiding in the baggage and begin living in your true identity. Identity's perception is about seeing and recognizing who God intends you to be.

Time might be the best measuring tool we have for understanding how much influence we allow God to have on our identity.

How much time do you spend perfecting your appearance each morning?
- 10 minutes
- 30 minutes
- 45 minutes
- More than 1 hour

How much time do you spend in God's Word and in prayer each morning?
- 10 minutes
- 30 minutes
- 45 minutes
- More than 1 hour

Psychologist Robert McGee wrote, "Separated from God and His Word, people have only their abilities and opinions of others on which to base their worth, and the circumstances around them ultimately control the way they feel about themselves."[iii] McGee continues, "…when we base our security on success and others' opinions, we become dependent on our abilities to perform and please others."[iv]

Read Psalm 139:13–14

> For you created my inmost being; you knit me together in my mother's womb. I praise you because I am fearfully and wonderfully made; your works are wonderful, I know that full well. (NIV)

How does God describe you in these verses?

_____
_____
_____

God made you. He has the best view of who you are. His opinion is the only one that matters, so change your perception of identity by understanding the only judgment that matters – God's opinion. If you spend time in His Word and in prayer, you will discover the truth of your identity. He isn't interested in all your accomplishments or how well you measure up to others. His perception of you is based on all the inner qualities that He put into your soul and mind. He knows those dreams and desires because He put them there. He knows your heart of compassion and love because He built these traits into you.

Changing your view and perception may be difficult, but with His help, you can become who God made you to be. In the space below, write a prayer asking God to motivate your attitudes and feelings instead of allowing the opinions of others to define you.

_____
_____
_____
_____
_____

Week One
Day Three
Identity's Creator

Today, let's look at three important and descriptive phrases from the psalm we read yesterday.

> For you created my inmost being; you knit me together in my mother's womb. I praise you because I am fearfully and wonderfully made; your works are wonderful, I know that full well (Psalm 139:13–14 NIV).

1. The first phrase is "You created my inmost being."

Almighty omniscient God created you. Imagine! Let's get a complete picture of what this phrase means.

Create means "to form or fashion, to produce, to bring something into existence." You were formed and fashioned by the Maker of the universe. You may have heard those words before, but the question is whether or not you believe it.

Identity begins with belief. I was created and you were created not by man, not with human hands, but by God's hands. Our Maker has divine wisdom, knowledge, ability, and capability. The same God who created the stars and the moon and the oceans and the land created you and created me.

God is an imaginative and ingenious creator. When He created animals, He provided them with everything needed to survive and thrive. The chameleon has the ability to change skin color as protection from predators. Some fish can blend in with the undersea environment to disguise their location.

He created the little bees, too, and gave them the instincts to engineer an air-conditioning system. When the weather gets hot and threatens to melt the wax in the hive, one group of bees goes to the entrance of the hive and another group stays inside. The bees flap and fan their wings in unison making a cross-draft that pushes the hot air out of the hive and draws cooler air inside.

God also made the human chromosome, which contains twenty billion bits of information. How much information is twenty billion bits? It would take more than four thousand textbooks to record twenty billion bits of information, yet God did it in one microscopic chromosome.

These examples are only a few of many illustrations we could use to point out the mighty and magnificent, intricate and detailed creation. The same God who created bees who make their own air conditioning created you. The same God who created a tiny, miniscule chromosome that houses billions of bits of information created you.

In the Psalm 139 passage, the language is figurative but it is clear that God has supernaturally watched over the natural process of reproduction in each of us. We are woven together with veins and arteries. God formed every detail of skeleton and frame and flesh and organs. And God prerecorded all the days of our lives before we were born. He marvelously planned every moment we would live. We are precious in God's view. Every day is relevant. He created us and He sustains us.[v]

Take a moment to let that sink in—the same God that created the universe created you and created me. And do you know what is most amazing? He considers us His greatest creation. Dwell on that thought for a moment. Write out your feelings about being made by the Master Creator.

_____
_____
_____
_____
_____
_____

2. The second phrase is "knit together in your mother's womb."

       Underline the word "knit."

Knitting requires much care, focus, and attention to detail. I remember trying to knit when I was a young girl. I watched my grandmother counting her stitches one by one. She took time with each project. Each stitch received deliberate attention; each thread was woven together in precise detail. Knitting requires a set pattern with various needles, stitches, and threading. The diverse components and designs make each piece unique.

In the same way, God's image is the pattern—the basis—of our design. Yet no two people have the same identical "stitch count." God uniquely and purposefully knit each one according to His design. From the moment God began to form you in your mother's womb, He had an expected end in mind.

God, in His great care, counted every stitch of your being. In fact, Jesus told his disciples, "Even the very hairs of your head are all numbered" (Matthew 10:30 NIV). I love my children very much, but I have not counted the number of hairs on their heads (nor do I intend to).

We were not casually formed by accident. Nothing was impromptu or impulsive about our design. God thoughtfully planned with full attention to every detail when He designed us.

What are some of your unique God-given features?

_____
_____
_____

3. The third phrase is "fearfully and wonderfully made."

Underline the phrase "fearfully and wonderfully made."

You may look in the mirror and see the wrong color hair or wish your nose was shorter. You may long to be taller or thinner, but when the God of the universe looks at you, He sees your perfect figure and face. God looks at you and He knows your ability and potential. Our Creator defines us not by our looks or our successes and defeats. We value ourselves by outward appearance or achievements, but our God, our Creator, does not.

At the close of a recent meeting, a woman approached me. I could see she had been crying. She explained, "As you spoke, I heard the words 'fearfully and wonderfully made' over and over in my mind."

"God must be speaking these wonderful words into your heart," I said.

"I've used that verse from the Psalms many times at baby showers to give encouragement to the mother-to-be." She continued, "But I never considered the idea for myself. I realize now that I am fearfully and wonderfully made."

She was so grateful to discover her own identity in the familiar verse when God opened her heart to believe the truth.

> For you created my inmost being; you knit me together in my mother's womb. I praise you because I am fearfully and wonderfully made; your works are wonderful, I know that full well (Psalm 139:13–14 NIV).

Do you believe this truth about yourself? Which of the three phrases from Psalm 139:13-14 are hard to believe? Which is easiest to accept?

_____
_____
_____
_____

Ask God to open your heart to the truth. *You* are created by God. God knit *you* together. *You* are fearfully and wonderfully made. *You* are His workmanship, and His works are wonderful.

Week One
Day Four
Identity's Purpose

Read Psalm 139:16:

> Your eyes saw my unformed body; all the days ordained for me were written in your book before one of them came to be (NIV).

What does this passage say about God's plan for your life?

_____
_____
_____
_____

All of our days were designed and intended by God before one of them came to be. There are no chance circumstances in our lives. Every detail is part of God's plan and process.

Some children are called a surprise addition to the family. Some people even refer to a child as an "accident child." Growing up feeling unwanted or unplanned harms children in ways psychologists are only beginning to understand. No matter what we have believed or been told, we are not an accident of nature. Almighty God created you and me. He planned the timing of your birth.

He planned each person with unique detail and design. He planned you. Everything about you. Think back to your list of identifying words again. Did you describe yourself with the phrase "made in God's image?"

In Genesis 1, God said,

> Let us [Father, Son and Holy Spirit] make mankind in Our image after Our likeness…. So God created man in His own image, in the image and likeness of God He created him; male and female He created them (Genesis 1:26-27 AMP).

God not only created us, He created us in His image. In the verse above, circle the words "created man in His own image."

God designed you for a purpose. The essence of what it means to be human beings created in the image of God is to learn who we are and why we are as well as what we are to do here on earth. "Failure to appreciate God's purpose for humanity has resulted in chaotic, purposeless thought and action. Ultimately, life without true knowledge of human nature as the image of God and human function as stewards of God's creation is life without a sense of meaning."[vi]

Understanding that you are created in His image is fundamental. By making us in His image, God gave us capacities not given to other forms of life.

Can you think of some of those capacities?

_____

_____

_____

He created us to think and reason and plan and dream. He imparts wisdom, knowledge, and capability to us. Our resemblance to Him is significant and vitally important. Understanding our image in Him answers questions about God's primary purpose for us.

Read Romans 11:36:

> For from him and through him and for him are all things. To him be the glory forever! Amen (NIV).

Everything finds its true meaning and purpose in God's meaning and purpose. He is the source and origin of our existence. He is our supreme purpose. He is our goal. He created all things, including you and me, for Himself and His pleasure. How contrary this is to our natural perspective.[vii] We live as though all things were from us, but all things are from Him. He made us to know Him and to love Him.

He has intentionally imprinted His divine image on you. God created us to be image bearers. This capacity means we can carry His image with us and project His characteristics to the world around us.

We are distinct from each other, yet each of us is made in the image of God our Creator. To visualize this concept, look into a mirror. Look at yourself for a few minutes without saying a word or moving a muscle in your face. Then, as you continue to gaze into the mirror, say, "I am looking at the image of God."

God is the ultimate focus. Next time you see a friend, try it. Look into her eyes and say, "I am looking at the image of God." See God's image as you sit around the dinner table with your family. Begin to appreciate yourself and others as persons who are made in God's image. If you are having difficulty believing how God sees you, read the following verses aloud. These may be well-known passages, but don't allow the familiarity to diminish the significance. Read the words as if you are hearing each one for the first time.

> How great is the love the Father has lavished on us, that we should be called children of God! And that is what we are! (1 John 3:1 NIV)

> For God so loved the world that he gave his one and only Son, that whoever believes in him shall not perish but have eternal life (John 3:16 NIV).

> I have been crucified with Christ and I no longer live, but Christ lives in me. The life I now live in the body, I live by faith in the Son of God, who loved me and gave himself for me (Galatians 2:20 NIV).

> The LORD does not look at the things people look at. People look at the outward appearance, but the LORD looks at the heart (1 Samuel 16:7b NIV).

Understanding how much God loves us and grasping His purpose for us should have an effect on how we treat or think about others and ourselves. When you understand and grasp how much God loves you, you will love others in a new and more purposeful way.

Read Romans 12:9-18:

> Love must be sincere. Hate what is evil; cling to what is good. Be devoted to one another in love. Honor one another above yourselves. Never be lacking in zeal, but keep your spiritual fervor, serving the Lord.

Be joyful in hope, patient in affliction, faithful in prayer. Share with the Lord's people who are in need. Practice hospitality.

Bless those who persecute you; bless and do not curse. Rejoice with those who rejoice; mourn with those who mourn. Live in harmony with one another. Do not be proud, but be willing to associate with people of low position. Do not be conceited.

Do not repay anyone evil for evil. Be careful to do what is right in the eyes of everyone. If it is possible, as far as it depends on you, live at peace with everyone (NIV).

You'll never recognize false identity until you recognize your true identity in God, and you will never live out the fullness of your identity until you have a clear, firm grasp on how God intends you to treat others. Be confident and secure in how you were made because confidence and security are developed from a pure sense of God-given identity. Then live in your maximum potential by ending focus on yourself and beginning directing your love and compassion to others.

Week One
Day Five
Identity's Role

The movie *Catch Me if you Can* depicts this concept. In the 1960s, Frank Abagnale Jr. successfully conned his way into millions of dollars using stolen identities. He fabricated eight different careers, including a Pan-Am pilot, doctor, and legal prosecutor. The movie portrays his plush lifestyle, but his wealth did not bring him stability or happiness. He was troubled with loneliness, constant hiding, and subsequent anxiety. Each time a name or role became useless or boring for his scams, he moved on to the next. The plot reveals how Frank's pursuit of money was rooted in his desire to solve his parents' marital problems. He thought financial instability had driven his mom away. This thought pushed him to become a con man. He constantly tried to get more money, thinking a large bank account would bring his mother home.

Sometimes we play a role instead of living in our true identity. There are obvious self-made roles such as a man who builds a great basketball career and takes great pride in his accomplishments. In a more subtle way, a role such as a caretaker who works with the elderly is still building an image as a "kind" person.

Whether obvious or subtle or both, we can resort to making much of ourselves. An award-winning basketball career and compassionate caretaking are not sinful. Both can be God-glorifying roles, but each one is a role—not an identity.

God is glorified when we put our roles in the right place, under His authority. And He is glorified when our grip is on Him and not on the role.

Make a list of your various roles. For example, mother, wife, schoolteacher, lawyer, etc.

_____
_____
_____
_____

We can have numerous roles yet still be undefined at the same time. Our identity is not in the roles we serve. Have you ever gotten your identity mixed up with your roles? Describe what happened.

_____
_____
_____
_____

I have muddled these two areas on more than one occasion. I have confused my role as a wife and mother with my identity. Confusing role and identity is easy to do and common among wives and mothers. Being a mom and wife are unlike other roles. When I close the computer, I put away my writer role. When I leave the platform, I've finished my role as speaker and I move on. But our role as a wife and a mother is a 24/7/365 role. So, of course, we can get confused. We can easily think, "This is who I am."

For example, if your child does not perform well or gets in trouble your heart aches and you certainly take steps to guide, direct, discipline, and love, but your identity is not in whether your child behaves correctly. Or if your role as a mother raising children becomes the mother with an empty nest, you might find yourself feeling worthless or invaluable. Your identity – the real, full, wonderful person God made you to be – isn't attached to your child. I am married to a brilliant, gifted, talented, godly man. We have been married for nearly thirty years. I have often wrapped my identity up in his. It's easy to do because I support and honor him, but his success shouldn't make or break me. Roles have a tremendous effect on true identity.

Now look back at your roles. Identify the ones you have made your identity.

_____
_____
_____

Read Psalm 139:13-14 again – aloud.

> For you created my inmost being; you knit me together in my mother's womb. I praise you because I am fearfully and wonderfully made; your works are wonderful, I know that full well (NIV).

You were fearfully and wonderfully made, created, and knit together *before* you ever had one of those roles. All of this took place in your mother's womb.

Keep in mind who God says you are and you will be a wonderful wife, mother, daughter, etc. One author said, "Don't forget to remember that you will never get from man what you can only get from God."[viii]

What unrealistic expectations have you put on your closest relationships?

_____

_____

Your husband, your children, and your friends can never complete your identity. Let them off the hook; only God can complete your identity. Allow God to direct your identity and then you can love, accept, nurture, develop, and make the most of your relationships.

When we try to build our identity from any outside source, we will be in a constant state of identity crisis.

Our identity must not be defined by possessions, achievements, physical attractiveness, public acclaim, roles, or people's opinions. When our concentration and attention center on the temporary things of life, whether they are good or bad, we become discontented because outward factors are subject to change.

Read Isaiah 40:8:

> The grass withers and the flowers fall, but the word of our God endures forever.

The prophet Isaiah made it clear that everything is fleeting *except* the Word of our God.

As you read the prophet's words, consider where you place your confidence. We often rely on our bank account balance, seniority, or personality strengths. According to Isaiah, what is the most permanent source of confidence?

_____

_____

_____

If I find my security, my acceptance, and my identity in any person or thing other than God, it's not going to last. I have become the victim of identity theft.

When we see that nothing else can support our identity, we're directed to the one thing that is our sure foundation.

Read Psalm 40:1-3:

> I waited patiently for the LORD; he turned to me and heard my cry.
> He lifted me out of the slimy pit, out of the mud and mire:
> He set my feet on a rock and gave me a firm place to stand.
> He put a new song in my mouth, a hymn of praise to our God.
> Many will see and fear the LORD and put their trust in him.

Let's live in our true identity. Living in our God-given identity influences every area of our lives.

****
GOING DEEPER

This week has been about discovering identity. We need to know our true identity before we can recognize the theft of it. Build your strength this week by reading these two passages of Scripture. Meditate and memorize each one.

Psalm 139:13–16:

> For you created my inmost being; you knit me together in my mother's womb. I praise you because I am fearfully and wonderfully made; your works are wonderful, I know that full well. My frame was not hidden from you when I was made in the secret place, when I was woven together in the depths of the earth. Your eyes saw my unformed body; all the days ordained for me were written in your book before one of them came to be (NIV).

Genesis 1:26–27:

> Then God said, "Let us make mankind in our image, in our likeness, so that they may rule over the fish in the sea and the birds in the sky, over the livestock and all the wild animals, and over all the creatures that move along the ground." So God created mankind in his own image, in the image of God he created them; male and female he created them (NIV).

Our identity and the source of our identity simply can't be disconnected. He created us, and in Him we discover who He intended us to be. In Him we discover our passion, our destiny, and our potential. Read the passages below and ponder the truth of God's plans for you.

Memorize one or two of these verses this week.

> "For I know the plans I have for you," declares the LORD, "plans to prosper you and not to harm you, plans to give you hope and a future" (Jeremiah 29:11 NIV).

> I know that you can do all things; no purpose of yours can be thwarted (Job 42:2 NIV).

LORD, you are my God; I will exalt you and praise your name, for in perfect faithfulness you have done wonderful things, things planned long ago (Isaiah 25:1 NIV).

Write a prayer thanking God for your identity.

_____
_____
_____
_____
_____

Week Two - God Approves of You

In Week One, we learned God created us. He not only created us, He gave us purpose and value. To know the significance of our worth and importance we need to understand that we are made in His image and after His likeness. In the Psalms, we discovered a beautiful but power-packed phrase: We are "fearfully and wonderfully made."

> For you created my inmost being; you knit me together in my mother's womb. I praise you because I am fearfully and wonderfully made; your works are wonderful, I know that full well (Psalm 139:13-14 NIV).

In those verses, we can clearly see our value. God Himself designed you. If you grasp the magnitude of that statement, you will begin to feel the value that God has placed on you.

The need for approval comes naturally to us. Watch any small child. She will draw a picture and as she shows it to you, she will breathlessly wait for you to admire it. "Do you like it, Mommy?" And if you are busy and say something like, "Yes, darling, that's nice," she won't be satisfied. "But did you see the colors and how I drew the butterfly and did you see the sun in the corner?" She will not stop until she is sure she has your total approval.

God approves of you. Even if you have made mistakes and even if those mistakes are big and seem unforgiveable. He made you. He knows your potential and He approves of you. He is your biggest cheerleader and encourager.

The great preacher John Ortberg wrote,

> When I catch myself comparing myself to others or thinking, *I could be happy if only I had what they have*, then I know I need to withdraw for a while and listen for another voice. Away from the winds, earthquakes, and fires of human recognition, I can again hear the still, small voice, posing the question it always asks of self-absorbed ministers: *What are you doing here?*

> I reply by whining about some of my own Ahabs and Jezebels. And the voice gently reminds me, as it has reminded thousands of Elijahs before me, that I am only a small part of a much larger movement, and at the end of the day there is only one King whose approval will matter.
>
> The voice also whispers, *Do not despise your place, your gifts, your voice, for you cannot have another's, and it would not fulfill you if you could.*[ix]

Ignore the fickle opinions of others and put away the nitpicky voices in your mind. Only the approval of God matters, and you have His endorsement, admiration, and love. He approves of you.

> Dear friends, if our hearts do not condemn us, we have confidence before God (1 John 3:21 NIV).

Week Two
Day One
Value

Fundamental to walking in our God–given identity is understanding that God values us. First, let's determine our value. Read the following verses.

Read 1 Corinthians 7:23:

> You have been bought and paid for by Christ, so you belong to him (NIV).

Read John 3:16:

> For God so loved the world that He gave His only begotten Son, that whoever believes in Him shall not perish but have everlasting life (NKJV).

What do these verses say about how much God values you?

_____
_____
_____
_____

Value is determined by what someone will pay. Jesus paid for your life with His death. He gave up His life for you. Don't underestimate your value to God. The cross proves your value and worth.

A friend wears a cross on a chain around her neck. It is a beautiful artistic creation made of the finest gold and exquisite precious stones. The cross has been passed down in her family for hundreds of years. It has an intrinsic value based on the current price of gold and diamonds, but it is priceless to her and her family.

If we hired an appraiser to place a value on the cross, she would base her opinion on the rarity of the piece, the popularity of the artist who designed it, and what price has been placed on other similar pieces. Jesus does not put a value on us with the methods of an appraiser. We are valuable to Him regardless of how we look or what talents we have. We are valuable to Him even if others do not value us.

My friend's cross has another value. It identifies her as a Christian. Many who follow Jesus wear a cross as a label. A mark recognized around the world. However, the deeper underlying value is not the gold or the stones or the sentimental importance. The real value of the cross is what it stands for. Jesus loves us so much that He paid the ultimate price—death. He loves you and values you.

Read Genesis 1:31:

> And God saw everything that He had made, and behold it was very good (suitable, pleasant) and He approved it completely (Genesis 1:31 AMP).

God created us. What was God's opinion about us as His creation?

_____
_____
_____
_____

God approved of His own handiwork. He looked at the human being and saw a good thing. I love how God expressed Himself. The wonderfully planned, God-imaged creation was good. Even more, it was *very* good.

God values you simply because you are His creation. There is nothing more you can do to increase your value, and there is nothing you can ever do to lose it.

Read Matthew 3:16-17 and 4:1:

> After being baptized, Jesus came up immediately from the water; and behold, the heavens were opened, and he saw the Spirit of God descending as a dove and lighting on Him, and behold, a voice out of the heavens said, "This is My beloved Son, in whom I am well-pleased" (NASB).

How does God describe His Son?

Think about the timing of the Father's words to His Son. When did God speak these words of affirmation over Jesus – the beginning, middle, or the end of his years of ministry?

These words were spoken on the eve of Jesus' public ministry. From the very beginning, God spoke His approval of His Son.

Consider these truths:

- Jesus received a strong affirmation of who He was **before** He began His ministry. God the Father acknowledged He was well pleased with Jesus as Jesus was baptized by John.
- Up to this point, Jesus hadn't performed a single miracle. No sign had been performed by Him, yet the Father said He was well pleased with His Son.
- Jesus hadn't successfully resisted the devil yet, but the Father opened the heavens and said, "This is My beloved Son, in whom I am well-pleased."

God said these loving words to Jesus before He had begun any work on earth. Jesus had not done one act of ministry. God approved Jesus. His value was not attained by what He did but by who He was.

Read Romans 5:8:

> But God demonstrates His own love toward us, in that while we were yet sinners, Christ died for us (NASB).

Did Jesus die for us based on our performance?

While we were in sin, Christ died for us. God values us so much that even in the midst of our sin, Christ died for us. Christ died for us not based on our performance but based on our God-given worth.

Imagine hearing the voice of God saying, "I am so very pleased with you." It is easy to fall into the trap of judging ourselves based on accomplishments, but God is pleased when we trust Him and believe Him by faith.

How does the fact that God values you make you feel?

_____
_____
_____
_____
_____

Does knowing you are pleasing and valuable to the Father help you feel free to do anything different today?

_____
_____
_____
_____

Think of your problems. Does getting a glimpse of your value give you new insight into how to face those difficulties? If so, describe how.

_____
_____
_____
_____
_____

Nothing we can do will make God esteem us more and nothing we could do will make God appreciate us less. He made us. His creation is perfect and He approves. Even if you have difficulty believing that God values you or you doubt He could forgive your failures, do not think, *God approves of everyone but me*. Nothing you can do will exclude you from God's love and approval.

In the space below, write what you think might disqualify you from God's approval.

_____
_____
_____
_____
_____
_____

Now strike through all those disqualifications and ask God to help you see yourself from His point of view. You are valuable. No price was too heavy for Him to pay for you. You are important and significant and useful to God.

Week Two
Day Two
Worth

Even when we comprehend and feel our value, we still have to make the transition from head knowledge to fully believing our worth.

Let's face it; we all want to feel valuable and worthy. I believe the yearning for worthiness is a God-given desire. We won't fully realize our worth if our primary focus is seeking meaning from other people. We are worthy because God says we are. We are worthy because we are created by God in His image. It is in knowing God that we establish our worth. If you don't know who God is, you will not know who you are. Confused identity could be avoided when we build our identity in Him. Put Him first and the second desire of feeling worthy will follow.

Another desire we have is for people to know and like us. It isn't wrong to want people to like you. In fact, God built us with the need for relationships, but no one ever achieved this desire by trying to be all things to all people or trying to meet everyone's expectations and win approval.

Derive your worth from what God says about you not what others say about you. Opinions from people are subjective, inconsistent, and emotional. Relying on other's opinions will make you insecure. Insecurity makes us difficult to get to know or want to be around.

People avoid those who are insecure and anxious and doubting. The cycle is vicious; by putting your opinion of me above God's opinion of me, I have put a second thing first. I lose my sense of worth of who I am in Christ and I not only lose friendships, I lose my intimacy with God.

When I believe I am who God says I am, I will become confident in the person He created me to be. True identity brings validity and vitality to relationships. If I find friendship with God first, friendships with others will develop naturally. Put first things first and the benefits will overflow.[x]

C.S. Lewis wrote about setting order to our lives. He used the terms first and second things.

> You never get second things by making them first things. You get second things by keeping first things first and then second things get thrown in.^{xi}

Sometimes we put the good and beneficial before our relationship with God. If any activity or relationship, no matter how noble or positive, takes priority over our intimacy with God, it will jeopardize our belief and deprive us of knowing our true worth to God.

Make a list of pursuits or relationships you may have put before your relationship with the Lord.

_____
_____
_____
_____

Make a commitment today to begin to put God first. Add a line at the top of this list and write the word, "God." Make Him a priority.

Deriving a worthy mindset can be challenging. Making God our priority helps. Developing a sense of our worth is particularly difficult if we have grown accustomed to negative words.

Some people have heard and believed negative words spoken to them. Words of disapproval make worthiness a very difficult truth to grasp. But your worthiness to God is the truth. Ask God to help you see clearly that He loves and approves of you. Brene Brown describes the battle of worthiness.

> The greatest challenge for most of us is believing we are worthy *now*, right this minute.
>
> - I'll be worthy when I lose 20 pounds.
> - I'll be worthy if I can get pregnant.
> - I'll be worthy if I can get/stay sober.

- I'll be worthy if everyone thinks I'm a good parent.
- I'll be worthy when my parents finally approve.
- I'll be worthy if he calls me back and asks me out.[xii]

Instead of trying to achieve or accumulate to be worthy, consider how much God values you.

Remember the verse from day one, Romans 5:8?

> But God demonstrates His own love toward us, in that while we were yet sinners, Christ died for us.

Complete your own "I'll be worthy when ..."

_____
_____
_____
_____

Then replace your negative thoughts with the words from Romans 5:8.

But God demonstrates His own love toward me, in that while I was _____, Christ died for me.

Remembering true worth comes from God is critical to living in God-given identity and will change your unworthy mindset.

We all feel unworthy at times. Let's read the story of Zacchaeus found in Luke 19:1-10.

> Then Jesus entered and passed through Jericho. Now behold, there was a man named Zacchaeus who was a chief tax collector, and he was rich. And he sought to see who Jesus was, but could not because of the crowd, for he was of short stature. So he ran ahead and climbed up into a sycamore tree to see Him, for He was going to pass that way. And when Jesus came to the place He looked up and saw him and said to him, "Zacchaeus, make haste and come down for today I must stay at your house." So he made haste and came down, and received Him joyfully. But when they saw it, they all complained, saying, "He has gone

to be a guest with a man who is a sinner." Then Zacchaeus stood and said to the Lord, "Look, Lord, I give half of my goods to the poor; and if I have taken anything from anyone by false accusation, I restore fourfold." And Jesus said to him, "Today salvation has come to this house, because he also is a son of Abraham; for the Son of Man has come to seek and to save that which was lost" (NKJV).

What kind of man was Zacchaeus?

_____

_____

What did Zacchaeus do when he heard Jesus was coming to town?

_____

_____

_____

What physical trait affected Zacchaeus' actions that day?

_____

What did Jesus do when He saw Zacchaeus in the tree?

_____

_____

_____

Pastor Rick Warren said, "I love the story of Zacchaeus. Zacchaeus was both a social and religious outcast. Everyone called Zacchaeus a sinner, but Jesus affirmed him and called him by his name 'pure one.' In the midst of negative public opinion and ridicule, Jesus affirmed Zacchaeus. When Jesus called Zacchaeus a son of Abraham, it was code for 'he's one of us, he's in the family'"[xiii]

How did Zacchaeus respond to Jesus?

_____

_____

_____

He sought Jesus. He fought the crowds. He did not let his bad reputation keep him away. And when Jesus called to him, Zacchaeus came down at once and went to Jesus. The encounter with Jesus changed Zacchaeus forever.

What physical or social trait makes you want to hide?

___

If you view yourself as unworthy, I encourage you to jump out of the tree where you are hiding. Come to Jesus. Not just when you feel worthy, but when you feel most unworthy. And not in confidence of what you have done, but in what Jesus has done for you.

Let Jesus change your view. When you believe Jesus loves and approves of you, it will change your unworthy mindset.

Week Two
Day Three
Choice

Yesterday we closed with the story of Zacchaeus. He made a choice to seek after Jesus. His choice changed his view of himself. We, too, must make that choice if we want to live in our true identity.

Read Matthew 6:33:

> But seek first the kingdom of God and His righteousness, and all these things shall be added to you (NKJV).

The present imperative verb "seek" makes clear that pursuing the kingdom of God and His righteousness are not passive or timid acts. Seeking God must be done with vigor and immediacy. Don't put it off. Pursue Him now. Or, if for some reason you've stopped seeking God, begin again.

How do you seek God?

_____
_____
_____

To help with this answer, think about the children of Israel. In the Old Testament, God led the children of Israel out of bondage in Egypt. God appeared to them in a pillar of cloud by day and a pillar of fire by night. Think about the position of the pillar. It was in front of them. In fact, the pillar of cloud shaded them from the hot desert sun so that they were kept cool during the day. At night, when the desert got very cold, God appeared in the fire, which gave them light as well as warmth. Whether He was the pillar of cloud or fire, He went in front of them.

As long as they followed Him, the Israelites did not have to worry about anything. God provided all their needs. He gave them water when they were thirsty and bread and meat when they were hungry. Their clothes did not wear out and their feet did not swell. They were kept in good health throughout the forty years of their wandering in the wilderness.

I sometimes wish I could see God that clearly. Imagine a pillar of fire to get you to your next destination. No question about whether God is leading – just follow the cloud. We don't have a cloud or pillar or a GPS signal to follow, but we can still watch for Him to show up in everyday experiences so we will know how and where to follow. If we are living in our true identity, we will choose to follow Him when we see signs of His presence.

Seeking God means you are on the lookout for God. You are looking for His guidance, His direction, His presence in your life. You wake up in the morning and turn your thoughts toward God. Throughout your day, in the midst of your daily routine and activity, you listen and look for God's direction. In the evening, you reflect on how He has been present and active in your life that day.

Tomorrow morning when you wake up, open your Bible. Ask Him for guidance for the day. Read the Word. You will discover direction and comfort and instructions. I can't count the number of times my morning Bible reading has directed my day. The verses may not seem meaningful as I read them at six in the morning, but later in the day when something comes up, God will bring the words to my memory. If one morning I read from Proverbs 15:1, "A gentle answer turns away wrath, but a harsh word stirs up anger," then later a co-worker says a hurtful thing, I can choose to remember the words I read and respond with kindness and peace. An unpleasant situation will be avoided and I will be living out my true identity in Jesus.

Seeking God is a choice. Pursuing and following God is a moment-by-moment and an all-day decision. Ultimately, it's a matter of trust. If I truly trust God, I will want to seek Him. I will want His guidance. I will desire His leadership.

Let's consider areas where we may have stopped seeking God. Look at the list below. Circle the disciplines that you may have fallen short in lately.

Quiet time	Bible reading
Giving	Worship
Caring for others	Meditation and prayer

Would you like to return to the Father in the areas you circled? He misses you and He longs for you. Begin now to take these disciplines up again and draw near to God, and He will draw near to you.[xiv]

Read Jeremiah 17:7-8:

> But blessed is the one who trusts in the Lord, whose confidence is in him. They will be like a tree planted by the water that sends out its roots by the stream. It does not fear when heat comes; its leaves are always green. It has no worries in a year of drought and never fails to bear fruit (NIV).

According to the prophet Jeremiah, what are the specific benefits of trusting in the Lord?

_____
_____
_____
_____

Did you write any of these words?

    Secure
    Sure
    Established

When we have made the choice to be firmly planted in the Lord, our attitude about our identity will change. We will trust God with the way He has designed us and be able to praise Him for the unique way He has knit us together.

Week Two
Day Four
Praise

When we fully understand our value and worth, we grasp just how much God approves of who we are. Yesterday we learned to pursue Him with right choices. All these discoveries lead us to praise.

Read Psalm 139:14:

> I praise you because I am fearfully and wonderfully made; your works are wonderful, I know that full well (NIV).

David praised God because of how he was created. According to this verse, how should we respond to God about our identity?

_____

_____

_____

We should praise God for creating us. I know the idea may sound arrogant or prideful, but in reality it is the opposite. God made us. Since we are created in His image, we all have gifts, abilities, talents, and attributes for which we should give Him the praise.

I'm a mother and I love to talk about our daughters. One daughter used to get so embarrassed when I talked about her abilities, until one day I explained, "Listen, I did not create you and neither did you create yourself. God made you; He made your brain. You are His creation. All the credit and all the glory goes to Him." My words helped her realize she shouldn't be uncomfortable about how God created her.

Read Psalm 139:14 again. This time in the New Living Translation.

> Thank you for making me so wonderfully complex!

Sometimes I think my husband would vote for a little less "complexity," but he wasn't casting a ballot when I was made. Our complexity makes us unique, and it is our responsibility to use what He has given us.

Read Philippians 3:12-14:

> Not that I have already attained or am already perfected, but I press on, that I may lay hold of that for which Christ Jesus has also laid hold of me. Brethren, I do not count myself to have apprehended; but one thing I do, forgetting those things which are behind and reaching forward to those things which are ahead, I press toward the goal for the prize of the upward call of God in Christ Jesus (NKJV).

What did Paul say about his responsibility?

_____
_____
_____
_____

Paul did not get hung up in an unworthy mindset. He's pressing on "flaws and all." He chose not to be inhibited by imperfect performance. He wanted to be found in Christ, to be like Him.

I don't believe God wants us to put ourselves down. Instead, He wants us to recognize the obligation of living in our true identity. Rather than put ourselves down, let's consider what we are accomplishing with the talents and abilities He has created in us.

What does Paul mean when he says to "press on?"

_____
_____
_____

What do you think it means to know Christ fully?

_____
_____
_____

How can we be transformed by Christ?

_____
_____
_____

As God's handiwork, I want to step up higher on every level. Knowing He made me is an encouragement to know Him, to listen to Him, and to obey Him. And I begin to understand the futility of comparison. There is no one else created exactly like me.

Knowing He loved me enough to individually form me with my own unique strengths makes me humbly bow before Him and say, "Thank you, Lord, for Your creation." Even when I see how He gave me my own special set of challenges, I realize He singled me out for a special purpose and I am irreplaceable in His creation.

Can you recall a testimony (maybe it is your own story) where unique or special challenges in a person's life were used to help the life of another?

_____
_____
_____
_____

There is no sense of pride in true identity. We had nothing to do with the creation.

But we do have a responsibility to live to the full potential of our image. If I think I am worthless and useless, I am dishonoring God and the identity He gave me. It's never too late to start faithfully pursuing and praising God – the One who designed you.

Accept the free gift of your creation in God according to His image and after His likeness and praise Him for it. What a privilege and opportunity to live out our image according to the truth. If you feel worthless, remember God's Spirit is ready and willing to work within you to make your identity all God intended it to be.

Read Philippians 1:6:

> ...being confident of this, that he who began a good work in you will carry it on to completion until the day of Christ Jesus (NIV).

What is Paul confident about?

_____
_____

God is going to complete the good work that He started. God will equip us to become all that He created us to be.

Accepting God's approval brings us to a crisis of belief and we will either believe God or we won't. He created you – believe it. You are fearfully and wonderfully made – believe it. You are made in His image – believe it. He accepts you perfectly and forgives you completely.

In the space below, write a praise to God for your identity.

_____
_____
_____
_____
_____
_____

You are a child of the Most High God. He approves of you and loves you.

Now personalize that sentence.

"I am a child of the Most High God. He approves of me and loves me."

I will praise and glorify Him for my identity.

Week Two
Day Five
Loved

We are loved. God, Creator of all, loves us immensely. His love is bigger and more loving than anything we can imagine.

Read John 15:13:

> Greater love has no one than this: to lay down one's life for one's friends (NIV).

What is the greatest kind of love?

_____

No love is greater than a sacrificial love. Jesus sacrificed His life for you. You are loved in the greatest way.

Read Jeremiah 31:3:

> I have loved you with an everlasting love; I have drawn you with unfailing kindness.

How long does God's love last?

_____

His love is not like anything we know on a human level because it is bigger and longer than any human love. Your identity is built on His love.

Read Psalm 139:17-18:

> How precious also are Your thoughts to me, O God! How great is the sum of them! If I should count them, they would be more in number than the sand; When I awake, I am still with You (NKJV).

The infinite mind of God thinks about us. One author said, "The thoughts of God toward us are altogether innumerable, for nothing can surpass the number of grains of sand. The task of counting God's thoughts of love would be a never-ending one. Even if we could count the sands on the seashore, we still would not be able to number God's thoughts, for they are 'more in number than the sand.'"[xv]

God thinks upon us infinitely. His extraordinary love and appreciation for you is part of your identity. He thinks of you continually and He approves of you just as you are.

We must remember this truth as we face the sometimes harsh realities of life. Some days there are situations that seem contrary to this truth.

It takes faith to believe how much God loves us, especially when we don't sense His presence. When life is tough, it is easy to doubt God's love and approval. It can be easy to think, *If God valued me, then…* or *If God loved me, then…*. When you are in the middle of a circumstance or situation and you desperately need to know that God is there, remember your identity. He values and loves you.

When our youngest daughter was two years old, I had her strapped in a car seat ready to pick up her sisters and the other neighborhood children from school. It was my day to drive carpool and we were waiting in the long line anticipating the older children rushing out of school to get into the car. All the carpool moms brought some sort of snack or treat, so I had a big jar of gumballs for the older children.

My daughter reached into the jar of gumballs and popped one into her mouth. All of a sudden, she started gagging; the gumball lodged in her throat. I grabbed her from the car seat and tried everything to dislodge the gumball, with no success. Everyone in the carpool line was anxious, and the school officials had been alerted. One mother saw what was happening and came to my aid. She was a pediatric nurse. It was if time stood still as I watched our precious daughter choking and grasping for air. After what seemed to be an eternity and several attempts, the nurse succeeded. The gumball was removed.

An ambulance arrived to transport us to the medical center. The nurses and doctors treated us with special care and attention, as if we had VIP status. We were amazed by the attention and extraordinary care at this large hospital. We learned later that the medical staff somehow thought our daughter was the niece of the chairman of the hospital.

I have no doubt these professionals would have treated our daughter and us in a loving, caring manner anyway, but they believed we were related to their boss, so we received exceptional attention and service.

Can you recall a time when you wondered if God was real or when you needed to know if He was present? Describe what happened.

_____
_____
_____
_____
_____

As God's child, you are special, too. He cares for you in every detail. His thoughts toward you are too numerous to count.

Read Ephesians 3:14-21:

> For this reason I kneel before the Father, from whom every family in heaven and on earth derives its name. I pray that out of his glorious riches he may strengthen you with power through his Spirit in your inner being, so that Christ may dwell in your hearts through faith. And I pray that you, being rooted and established in love, may have power, together with all the Lord's holy people, to grasp how wide and long and high and deep is the love of Christ, and to know this love that surpasses knowledge—that you may be filled to the measure of all the fullness of God. Now to him who is able to do immeasurably more than all we ask or imagine, according to his power that is at work within us, to him be glory in the church and in Christ Jesus throughout all generations, for ever and ever! Amen (NIV).

Circle the words "wide," "long," "high," and "deep." In your own words below, write how these four words express the love of God.

_____
_____
_____
_____
_____

According to these verses, how much can God do?

_____
_____
_____

In the space below using phrases from this verse, write a prayer expressing the affirming power of God's love.

_____
_____
_____
_____
_____
_____
_____

****
GOING DEEPER

In Week One we tried to grasp the origin, source, and purpose of true identity. This week we have worked to understand our response to God's amazing love in giving us a special, unique identity. I have determined to seek God and believe in my worth and value. I hope you will seek Him, too. We will praise God for our unique identity and let God's love and approval roll over us.

For many, this lesson of God's approval may have been a difficult one to grasp. Comprehending the love and acceptance of God is hard because we know too much about ourselves and our disappointments and failures. Fully accepting His approval is the key to walking in our identity. Spend some time this week re-reading Ephesians 3:14-21. Memorize your favorite part of this Scripture.

> For this reason I kneel before the Father, from whom every family in heaven and on earth derives its name. I pray that out of his glorious riches he may strengthen you with power through his Spirit in your inner being, so that Christ may dwell in your hearts through faith.
>
> And I pray that you, being rooted and established in love, may have power, together with all the Lord's holy people, to grasp how wide and long and high and deep is the love of Christ, and to know this love that surpasses knowledge—that you may be filled to the measure of all the fullness of God.
>
> Now to him who is able to do immeasurably more than all we ask or imagine, according to his power that is at work within us, to him be glory in the church and in Christ Jesus throughout all generations, for ever and ever! Amen (NIV).

In the space below, write a prayer using phrases and words from the Ephesians passage.

_____
_____
_____
_____

Read 1 John 3:1-2:

> Consider this: The Father has given us his love. He loves us so much that we are actually called God's dear children. And that's what we are. For this reason the world doesn't recognize us, and it didn't recognize him either. Dear friends, now we are God's children (GW).

Memorize these two verses. Say them aloud each morning as you rise up from bed.

Week Three - Characteristics of Your God-given Identity

If you lost your personal identity, experts would give you specific steps to repair the damage inflicted by an identity theft. A financial expert would help you reestablish your credit worthiness; a computer mastermind might help you construct un-hackable passwords; a banker could open new accounts and give you guidelines for protecting your passwords, account numbers, and personal information.

Ask any woman about a beautiful antique in her home and you'll likely hear the story of how she found the old piece in a junk pile. It probably had ten coats of paint and might have been broken or was missing a leg. Then she took it to a restoration expert who gently removed the layers of peeling and cracked paint and repaired the damaged parts. After carefully and lovingly sanding and smoothing it, the piece was fully restored to the vintage beauty you've admired.

When it comes to your spiritual identity, there is no better expert than God. He created you and built your character strengths and personality traits. He is the inventor and designer of your identity and knows you like no one else. If the enemy has stolen your identity or made you feel less than your whole self, God will restore you.

From the beginning God knew how crafty and evil our enemy can be. Before you were born God set a plan in motion to redeem and restore you. God created you and gave you a unique and distinctive identity. Nothing is too hard for Him. No matter what has happened to you, He restores fully and completely.

Week Three
Day One
Redeemed

Since the Garden of Eden, every person has inherited a sinful nature. Our initial identity theft came at birth. Everyone who has ever been born has a problem with sin.

Read Romans 3:23:

> For all have sinned and fall short of the glory of God (NIV).

Who has sinned?

_____

We are all victims of sin, but God has provided a way of salvation. Neither does God leave us as victims of identity theft. He has made a way for us to live in our full image-bearing potential.

We can get back our true identity. He has provided a way. The theological word is redemption.

Read Romans 3:24:

> [All] are justified and made upright and in right standing with God, freely and gratuitously by His grace (His unmerited favor and mercy), through the redemption which is [provided] in Christ Jesus (AMP).

Define redemption.

_____

Who qualifies for redemption?

_____

Do we earn it?

_____

_____

Redemption is a comprehensive and wide-ranging concept. It means:

- Make something acceptable or pleasant in spite of its negative qualities or aspects
- Restore reputation – changes a negative opinion to a positive one
- Buy back an item
- Fulfill a pledge or promise
- Pay off a debt

Jesus redeems our identity. He restores, repairs, replaces, and renovates our status. Jesus bought back our true identity from the thief. But redemption is even better than that. Jesus didn't just buy it back. He bought it because He wants to give it back to you. Your identity has been purchased by Christ on the cross. Now He offers redemption to you as a free gift. Ask Him. He gives freely.

Read Romans 10:13:

> For whosoever calls upon the name of the Lord will be saved (KJV).

You can be saved from identity theft by calling on the name of Jesus. You can be saved from an existence based on a lie. False identity is destroyed. True identity is revealed. False things are made true.

If you haven't called on the name of Jesus, let me encourage you to stop right now and cross the line of faith. Receive the gift of redemption.

Share about the time in your life when you accepted the redemption of Jesus. Do you remember the time? Place? Special circumstance?

_____

_____

_____

_____

Fifteen years ago I began a new Bible study course with a group of what I thought were all mature Christ followers who had well-worn Bibles. In one of the first sessions, a forty-five-year old woman named Marcia asked the Bible study leader, "What does the word 'sanctification' mean?"

A little surprised by the question, the leader asked if Marcia knew what being saved meant. Marcia looked confused and quietly answered, "No."

Marcia grew up in a traditional religious home but left the Catholic Church at the age of eighteen. As she became an adult, she decided that being a Christian meant being a good person, so she tried to do right and behave well. She had never read the Bible, so she had a counterfeit and corrupted view of who God is. She wasn't so sure God was real or good; she feared the boom of punishment would be lowered at any moment. She had absolutely no idea that God intended us to have a personal relationship with Him. Or that her identity was wrapped up in God's love for her. Furthermore, she thought no one could know where you stand with God—whether you were "thumbs up" or "thumbs down."

The study leader quickly and gently responded to Marcia by reading several verses from the book of Romans, verses often referred to as the Roman Road. These verses reveal that all have sinned and the wages of sin is death. But God had a desire and plan for each person to be rescued and He provided for salvation through Jesus' death on the cross. Jesus died in our place to take on our sins, and we receive the free gift of salvation by putting our faith in Jesus as our personal Lord and Savior.

Marcia recognized the truth as the leader read the verses. She said, "The truth hit me with the force of a Mac truck. For forty-five years I had been drifting on a dark planet and in that bright and glorious instant, the light of salvation illuminated my path and changed everything."

Marcia made an earnest confession of faith and as tears streamed from her eyes, she accepted the gift of God and felt deep gratitude for God's goodness and greatness.

For forty-five years, the enemy stole her identity, her rightful position as a royal daughter in God's family. But in that appointed moment in time, her true identity was revealed, and she claimed her glorious, God-given inheritance. Through grace, she received an eternal garment of righteousness in exchange for rags of sin and self-reliance she unwittingly wore for forty-five years. Just as you would expect, from that moment on, God began the process of radical transformation (sanctification) from the inside out.[xvi]

Read Romans 5:17-18:

> For the sin of this one man, Adam, caused death to rule over many. But even greater is God's wonderful grace and his gift of righteousness, for all who receive it will live in triumph over sin and death through this one man, Jesus Christ.
>
> Yes, Adam's one sin brings condemnation for everyone, but Christ's one act of righteousness brings a right relationship with God and new life for everyone (NLT).

We were lost and beyond hope. But when Christ gave His life, He redeemed us. He bought us back. He claimed us. He gave us back our true identity.

Week Three
Day Two
Righteous

Death and unrighteousness came into all mankind through Adam, but the gift of righteousness and life comes through Christ Jesus to those that receive Him. Righteousness is a part of our restored identity.

Yesterday we ended with the verses from Romans 5, which showed us how Jesus redeemed us and through that redemption, He gave us righteousness.

Righteousness means that we are right before God and in right standing with Him. He sees us through the righteousness that Jesus imparted to us at the cross. From the moment you placed your faith in Jesus Christ, your heart was stamped with the blood of Christ. You are cleared of sin and condemnation in the eyes of God. Jesus' record replaces your record. And even though we continue sinning while here on earth, our eternal record is forever changed. When God looks at believers, He sees the imprinted image of Christ. What a miracle! When God looks down, He sees me as fully righteous, because He has made me righteous.

I have received redemption and my heart and soul are changed forever. I love God and revel in His love and sacrifice. But I still live in a fallen world. I make mistakes, I sin, and I fail.

We can't seem to live up to His glorious eternal standard in our mortal bodies. Here and there in daily living we have allowed Satan to trick us and push us away from our God-given character and heritage.

We need to reclaim the righteousness redemption gave us.

Read 2 Corinthians 5:17:

> Therefore, if anyone is in Christ, he is a new creation; old things have passed away; behold, all things have become new (NKJV).

According to this verse what has passed away?

_____
_____
_____
_____

We have to believe and act on who God says we are. In Christ Jesus, we have a new identity.

Read Romans 5:17 again:

> But even greater is God's wonderful grace and his gift of righteousness, for all *who receive it will live in triumph over sin and death* through this one man, Jesus Christ (emphasis mine).

Because of redemption, we can live righteous lives. In triumph, because of Jesus.

Read 2 Corinthians 5:17 again:

> Therefore, if anyone is in Christ, he is a new creation; old things have passed away; behold, all things have become new.

Read John 8:32:

> And you shall know the truth, and the truth shall make you free (NKJV).

What is the benefit of knowing the truth?

_____
_____
_____

The word "know" means "to perceive, understand, recognize, gain knowledge, or come to know." When we come to know Him, we gain greater understanding of our identity. We perceive His truth and feel His freedom. It is a progressive knowledge. The more we know of Him, the freer we are to live in our true identity.

The enemy's accusing voice seeks to defeat us by telling us we should already know the answers. He may whisper, "You have been to church and you aren't cured. It didn't work that time, so it's not going to work now. If God cared, you would be over this struggle."

Describe a recurring struggle in your life.

_____
_____
_____
_____
_____
_____

The enemy is a half-truth teller (thus, a liar). I may still be facing the same situation again, but I know my identity because I know the identity-giver. God is the source of my identity, and He has given me His word about who I am. That truth is found in God's Word and fuels our true identity and maintains our true image. And to truly grasp this concept we must not treat God's Word like any other human advice. The Bible is the source of our identity and the foundation for which we can firmly grasp who we are. Your life matters, and your identity counts.

Laura is my dear friend and longtime Bible teacher. She knows the Word and lives it, but knowing her true identity didn't come easy or naturally for Laura.[xvii]

As you read her testimony, notice how the powerful Word of God has shaped her life. Underline anything in her testimony that reminds you of your own struggle. Look up and meditate on the Scriptures references. Allow the truth to shape your identity.

Laura's Story

> In God's prefect way, His truth completely changed my life. I am a child of divorce, a product of what was then called a "broken home." When my father left our family, my heart indeed was broken. I felt rejected and abandoned. My life and my identity as my daddy's girl were shattered. But in God's infinite wisdom and perfect plan, He used this life-shattering event to call me to Himself and turned it into a life-changing event.

When a Sunday school teacher told me about God's promise to be a father to the fatherless (Psalm 68:5), the Holy Spirit burned within me, calling me to a saving relationship with God, the Father, through Jesus Christ, His Son. I knew, as the Holy Spirit ministered this truth to my six-year-old heart and mind, that apart from Jesus, I could not have relationship with God because of my sin. I knew that I needed to be saved from my sin and that Jesus was the One that gave His life as a payment for my sin. In that one moment of truth I prayed and asked Jesus to be my Savior and Lord.

He changed my identity from broken little girl to child of Almighty God. Jesus set me on a path of discovery where I would learn how to live out the reality of who I am in Christ. Has it been an easy journey? No, but it has been the most rewarding, most exhilarating experience of my life.

As I matured, learning to live out of my new identity proved a challenging assignment. During the difficult times of my childhood, I had internalized the deep emotional pain caused by the circumstances, and I struggled with the wounds of rejection and abandonment. Eventually, as a young wife, I crashed emotionally. One day, in desperation, I cried out to the Lord, for I knew He was my Hope and my Healer. He opened my eyes to see my wounded soul and offered healing and wholeness. I desperately wanted to be free of the rejection and to walk in the newness of life promised in Romans 6:4. It sounds humorous now, but as I cried and cried in those dark days, I held on to my Bible and prayed for answers.

I knew the answers were in the Word. But where? There's no listing in the concordance for "young wife falls apart." But God, as always, was faithful.

I loved Jesus with everything in me, but I did not know how to live wholly out of the riches of His grace. I started reading John 14, "If anyone loves Me, he will keep My word; and My Father will love him, and We will come to him and make our abode with him… (and) the Helper, the Holy Spirit, Whom the Father will send in My name, He will teach you all things and bring to your remembrance all that I said to you" (John 14:23, 26). There it was as plain as can be: to love and know God is to learn, remember, and obey all that He has said.

From that time on, I developed a thirst for knowing His truth and just as in Psalm 42, my soul longed for and thirsted for God. I began to study the Word, examining every thought and attitude of my heart and measuring them against what God said is right and true. Through time in the Word, I saw in myself attitudes and behaviors that were in opposition to God and I learned to treasure the mercy and grace of repentance, confession, and forgiveness.

It was and still is an amazing experience to be transformed by the renewing of my mind through the power of the Holy Spirit as He ministers the truth to me through the Word. The Word restores my soul, makes me wise, rejoices my heart, enlightens my eyes, keeps me from sin, and endures forever (Psalm 19). It challenges and comforts me, strengthens and sustains me. It tells me the truth about who I am—I am loved! I am treasured! I am His!

Knowing and choosing to live out of the truth of God's Word has completely changed me! And He will do the same for anyone who believes and truly desires to know, accept, and apply His truth.

Read the last paragraph of Laura's testimony again.

Now look back at your list of struggles on page 63. Ask God to show you the truth about each one of those struggles.

_____
_____
_____

Week Three
Day Three
Restored

If we believe His Word, we will be secure in our true identity. But it is a choice we have to make. If we base our identity on something other than the Word of God, we often center our identity on how we feel. I don't feel righteous; therefore, although God tells me I am righteous, I can't possibly be righteous. Do you trust in God's Word rather than the evidence of your circumstances or emotions?

The Bible is true; the Bible is reliable. The Bible reveals to us who we really are.

Read 2 Timothy 3:16:

> Every scripture inspired of God is also profitable for teaching, for reproof, for correction, for instruction, which is in righteousness (NASV).

Place a check by the following question or questions which describe your situation and the words you say to yourself.

- ☐ Do memories remind you of failures or poor performance in your past? (I'm a failure.)

- ☐ Do you consider yourself less than perfect or unworthy because of past mistakes and rebellion? (I'm unworthy.)

- ☐ Do you let those old sins hang over your head and breathe down your neck? (I'm condemned.)

- ☐ Are worries about future circumstances overtaking your thoughts? (I'm anxious.)

- ☐ Do finances or job prospects control you? (I'm in control.)

☐ Does the future of your children trouble you? (I'm afraid.)

☐ Is there a problem with your relationships? (I'm insecure.)

☐ Does your career demand all your energy or do the expectations of the boss overwhelm? (I'm powerless.)

If you checked any of the items above, you have allowed outside sources to dictate your identity and your future. It is time you allowed the presence of God to breathe into your life and to help you understand how precious you are to Him. Ask yourself this: Who's breathing on me? In other words, who or what voice do you allow to whisper in your ear?

When I was pregnant with our first daughter, Duncan and I attended pre-birthing classes. We wanted to do everything we could to have the best labor and delivery, so we carefully listened to the experts. Duncan was instructed to remind me to breathe at a certain point in the labor process. He was encouraged to breathe with me—to imitate slow, controlled breathing. On August 3, that's exactly what he did. During one of the major birth contractions, he leaned over me and said, "Breathe, Honey." He demonstrated the breathing technique. At that moment, I experienced a major contraction. All I could do was look at him and with a voice that would scare the devil himself, I shouted, "Don't breathe on me!"

It is important to decide who or what we will allow to breathe on us. How do we function in our identity? By breathing in the right thing. Let's look back at how we were created.

Read Genesis 2:7:

> The LORD God formed a man from the dust of the ground and breathed into his nostrils the breath of life, and man became a living being (NIV).

How did God bring Adam and Eve into being?

_____

_____

God brought life to us through His breath and taught us how to breathe. He put His air into our lungs, and it is the breath of the Creator that brought us life. What can be more intimate than the breath of God giving us life? We took our first breath because the creator of the universe, Almighty God, gave it to us. There is something so personal about that picture. He could have given us life by any means. He chose to breathe on us. God's breath gave life to our image.

We were formed in His image and received his life-giving breath. We need the breath of life to live out our full image-bearing capacity and potential. We need His breath not only for gaining our initial identity, but also for maintaining our identity. Without His breath, our weary heart is prone to falter back to its previous ways.

Think about a newborn baby. The continual breathing of a newborn baby promotes tissue formation. If a newborn has difficulty breathing, she is at risk for becoming a "blue baby" due to low oxygenated blood. Feeling blue is also our default without the Lord's breath. We end up anxious, depressed, and overwhelmed.

Consider how the "breath" of others is influencing you today. If being around a certain person causes you to feel blue, you might need to consider whether that person should be an influencer over your life. If you feel anxious, frustrated, or overwhelmed, perhaps you need to read the Psalms or other comforting passages of Scripture that will give you peace and cause your faith to grow stronger. If you feel unworthy or as if you have failed, go back to weeks one and two in this study and reaffirm the love and provision of God.

Sometimes we let the noise around us influence our soul. Look at the list below and honestly evaluate whether you are allowing any of these to breathe on you. We've placed check boxes beside each item on the list because we believe it is helpful to acknowledge how these common activities shape us. Check the ones that you regularly allow to influence you.

- ☐ Mindless sit-coms on TV
- ☐ Tedious political news
- ☐ Gratuitous novels
- ☐ Slightly off-color movies
- ☐ Time-consuming Internet surfing
- ☐ Inappropriate relationships

Bad breath is all around us, but we don't have to let it breathe on us. There is a better option. The choice is up to us.

When treating a drowning victim, emergency medical technicians begin to pump in fresh air while flushing out the water. God does the same with us. He breathes life and fullness into our lives through the Word and prayer, and as we are filled with the energy of His love and power, the corrupt and wicked things of our enemy are flushed out.

Physical breath circulates throughout our system and moves vital nutrients and oxygen to our lungs and brains. Breath helps blood flow to our arms and legs and keeps us moving and alive. The breath of God also spreads throughout every pore to bring us restoration.

Week Three
Day Four
Responsive

God is still breathing His life into each of us.

Read 2 Timothy 3:16:

>All Scripture is God-breathed (NIV).

Our first response to God's breath is to read and take in the Word of God. Scripture is God-breathed and His good breath flows from the Word. Every time you read His Word, every time you hear a Scripture, God breathes on you and into you. God's Word brings His image in you and in me. Our identities will not only be restored and redeemed, but if we spend significant time reading and meditating on His Word, we put ourselves into a position to hear Him. When we hear Him, we can respond with enthusiasm, passion, and joy.

No one can do this work for you. You decide to allow God to breathe life and health and hope and joy into you. If you don't intentionally put God into the position of influence, something else will fuel your life. The enemy.

Listen carefully to the Word of God. Open your ears to what He is saying. Pay close attention. Carefully listen and be diligent. Let the Word breathe life into you.

Don't open your ears, your mind, or your heart to everything you hear. Even if you hear it from a good friend. Test it against the Word of Truth, God's Word. We live as victims of identity theft because we inhale lies and believe everything we hear. Guard your ears. Set your mind on things of God and keep it set on the truth.

There is only one reliable, unchanging, everlasting, true source that you can trust when it comes to your identity, and that one source is the Word of God.

A few days ago we discussed how Paul moved forward "flaws and all." Read the following verses and then on the lines provided, describe some of Paul's imperfections.

1 Timothy 1:16-17:

> But God had mercy on me so that Christ Jesus could use me as a prime example of his great patience with even the worst sinners. Then others will realize that they, too, can believe in him and receive eternal life. All honor and glory to God forever and ever! He is the eternal King, the unseen one who never dies; he alone is God. Amen (NLT).

1 Corinthians 15:9:

> For I am the least of the apostles and do not even deserve to be called an apostle, because I persecuted the church of God (NIV).

Ephesians 3:8:

> Although I am less than the least of all the Lord's people, this grace was given me: to preach to the Gentiles the boundless riches of Christ.

_____
_____
_____
_____
_____
_____
_____

Paul is the extreme example. Paul had been a great persecutor of the church and even called himself the "worst of sinners." Yet God changed that old identity of Paul into the greatest apostle. The worst sinner whose identity has been rescued responded in such a way to become the greatest saint. Nothing you have done will prevent God from redeeming and rescuing you. Your decision is how you will respond to His grace and patience.

> Christians have always struggled with grace. It's far easier for us to accept the reality that a holy God hates our sin than it is for us to really believe that He can use flawed instruments to fulfill His perfect design. For some reason, we're reluctant to believe He loves us, forgives us, and truly wants what's best for us, even when we sin.[xviii]

The Bible is full of examples of men and women who responded to God even though the enemy had stolen their identity. Elijah became so afraid of Jezebel that he ran in fear. Jonah hated the Ninevites so much that he refused to go to the wicked city to tell of God's love. Even Paul's contemporaries preached the gospel with unworthy motives because they didn't identify with the truth of Jesus. Yet God used each one to spread the Gospel and save nations. Our identity may be compromised, but God's love and purpose for us is never thwarted.

Read 2 Corinthians 12:9:

> But he said to me, "My grace is sufficient for you, for my power is made perfect in weakness." Therefore I will boast all the more gladly about my weaknesses, so that Christ's power may rest on me."

What is made perfect in weakness?

_____

When Paul heard these words from Jesus, what was Paul's response?

_____
_____
_____
_____

God uses flawed instruments to accomplish His work. Our loss of identity is no excuse to sin or grumble. Our response is to trust God and resist the enemy so we can live in our true identity.

Response comes in various forms. A second form of response is praise. Praise is a major response to combat identity theft. Praise God for all His blessings. Praise God for His unconditional love. Praise God for the past (even the difficult times) and for the present and for the future.

Praise is not denying your feelings or your circumstances. There are times when the circumstances are bleak and our efforts have failed. Our identity can be shaken. Discouragement and disappointment are real. The Bible is clear about how we should handle those times.

Read Psalm 42:11:

> Why, my soul, are you downcast? Why so disturbed within me? Put your hope in God, for I will yet praise him, my Savior and my God.

What are we to do when disturbed?

_____
_____

Read Hebrews 13:15:

> Through Jesus, therefore, let us continually offer to God a sacrifice of praise—the fruit of lips that confess his name.

What are we encouraged to do when we are discouraged and disappointed?

_____

Praise in the midst of the circumstance. It's not easy. It's called a sacrifice of praise. A sacrifice indicates your feelings or your circumstances are not conducive to praise.

God loves us and offers His hope and peace in every situation. Our job is to respond to Him. When disturbed, our response should be to put our trust in Him. He is able. We can fully rely on Him even when the situation looks impossible. When we are discouraged or disappointed, the answer is not to whine or complain. The correct response is to praise Him. To say His name. To call on His name aloud and believe His Word.

Read these verses from Psalm 145 and underline all the reasons you can find to praise the Lord.

> The LORD is gracious and compassionate, slow to anger and rich in love.
> The LORD is good to all; he has compassion on all he has made.
> All your works praise you, LORD; your faithful people extol you.

Your kingdom is an everlasting kingdom, and your dominion endures through all generations. The LORD is trustworthy in all he promises and faithful in all he does.

The LORD upholds all who fall and lifts up all who are bowed down.

You open your hand and satisfy the desires of every living thing.

The LORD is righteous in all his ways and faithful in all he does

The LORD is near to all who call on him, to all who call on him in truth.

He fulfills the desires of those who fear him; he hears their cry and saves them.

The LORD watches over all who love him, but all the wicked he will destroy.

My mouth will speak in praise of the LORD. Let every creature praise his holy name forever and ever.

A characteristic of our God-given-identity is responsive praise. Look at the words you underlined and write them in the space below.

_____
_____
_____
_____
_____
_____

Whenever you feel your identity slipping away or you wonder if your life has purpose and meaning, stop the negative thinking with praise. Praising God for all He is and for all He has done will change your heart and attitude. Admire Him. Applaud Him. Worship Him. Praising Him will remind you of your true identity.

Week Three
Day Five
Re-focused

Yesterday we learned ways to respond to our identity. We respond to His Word, and we respond with praise.

Today we will talk about our focus and how we can stay focused on our God-given identity.

Read Psalm 107:2:

> Let the redeemed of the LORD say so, whom he has redeemed from trouble (RSV).

What are we supposed to do if the Lord has redeemed us?

_____

_____

_____

Has the Lord redeemed you? Then speak out. Jesus has redeemed us, so let's line our mouth up with the truth. Get in agreement with God. Jesus redeemed your identity. Believe the truth about your identity and speak the truth to your soul.

Consider whether you are using the words you speak and the words in your mind as truth-bearers.

If memories remind you of failures in your past or if you base your identity on your poor performance, you might say, "I'm a failure."

Instead, believe Romans 8:37:

> No, in all these things we are more than conquerors through him who loved us (NIV).

And say,

> "I may have failed, but I'm not a failure. Because Jesus lives in me, I am more than a conqueror."

If you consider yourself less than perfect or unworthy because of past mistakes and rebellion, you might say, "I'm unworthy."

Instead, believe Romans 8:1:

> There is therefore now no condemnation for those who are in Christ Jesus (NRSV).

And say,

> "I may have rebelled, but I'm not unworthy. Jesus has made me worthy."

If old sins seem to hang over your head and breathe down your neck, you might say, "I'm condemned."

Instead, believe 2 Corinthians 5:21:

> I am the righteousness of God in Jesus Christ (paraphrase).

And say,

> "I may have sinned, but I am not a sinner. I am in right standing with God."

If worries about future circumstances overtake your thoughts, you might say, "I'm anxious."

Instead believe, Philippians 4:4-7:

> Rejoice in the Lord always; again I will say, rejoice. Let your reasonableness be known to everyone. The Lord is at hand; do not be anxious about anything, but in everything by prayer and supplication with thanksgiving let your requests be made known to God. And the peace of God, which surpasses all understanding, will guard your hearts and your minds in Christ Jesus (ESV).

And say,

> "I may have cares, but I'm not anxious. I am peaceful because God has my concerns."

If finances or job prospects control you, you might say, "I'm in control."

Instead, believe Philippians 4:19:

> And my God will meet all your needs according to his glorious riches in Christ Jesus (NIV).

And say,

> "My resources may be limited, but I'm not in control. All my needs are supplied by God according to His riches."

If you are troubled about the future of your children you might say, "I'm afraid."

Instead, believe Isaiah 41:10:

> Don't be afraid, for I am with you. Don't be discouraged, for I am your God. I will strengthen you and help you. I will hold you up with my victorious right hand (NLT).

And say,

> "I may have doubts, but I'm not afraid. I am confident God is with me giving me His strength and His help."

If there is a problem in one of your relationships, you might say, "I'm insecure."

Instead, believe Colossians 3:12:

> I am His elect, full of mercy, kindness, humility, and longsuffering (paraphrase).

And say,

> "Relationships aren't perfect, but I'm secure. I am God's chosen one filled with his mercy, kindness, humility, and longsuffering."

If your work demands all your energy and the career and expectations of your boss feel overwhelming, do not say, "I'm powerless."

Instead, believe Galatians 2:20:

> It is no longer I who live, but Christ lives in me (NLT).

And Philippians 4:13:

> I can do all things through him who strengthens me (NRSV).

And say,

> "I may be tired, but I'm equipped. Christ lives in me and gives me strength."

Ask God to show you any other thoughts or patterns of thinking that do not line up with your redeemed identity. Ask Him to reveal His truth to you about each of these areas. Ask Him to heal those areas where you have believed lies.

Confessing your righteousness in Christ keeps you conscious of Jesus. It does not matter how many sermons or books on righteousness you have heard and read. You need to believe it and speak it.

Every time you speak it, you magnify His finished work on the cross. So believe and speak the truth.

A common claim is that we cannot change the way we feel. But when we change the way we think, it will change the way we speak and act. Feelings follow thoughts and actions.

Refocusing our thinking and the words we say will change us. We will rediscover our true identity in Christ, and we may uncover dreams and longings that the enemy crushed in his attempt to steal our identity.

Mark Batterson said, "A big dream is simultaneously the best feeling and worst feeling in the world. It's exhilarating because it's beyond your ability; it's frightening for the same exact reason."[xix]

If the enemy has stolen your dream along with your identity, you can once again open the windows of opportunity and vision by taking your eyes off your problems and refocusing on God and the future God has planned for you.

****
GOING DEEPER

This week we have established five of the characteristics of walking in your true identity, five important features that are an integral part of your identity. You are redeemed – purchased by the blood of the Lamb. You are righteous – not your own righteousness but His bestowed on you. You are restored – no longer a false individual but living in your true original identity. You are responsive – aware of God's work in your life and ready to follow Him. You are re-focused – paying attention to His voice in your life and speaking the truth over your life.

Paul believed we can walk in our true identity. In fact, he prayed for the Colossian people.

Read Colossians 1:9-11:

> For this reason, since the day we heard about you, we have not stopped praying for you. We continually ask God to fill you with the knowledge of his will through all the wisdom and understanding that the Spirit gives, so that you may live a life worthy of the Lord and please him in every way: bearing fruit in every good work, growing in the knowledge of God, being strengthened with all power according to his glorious might so that you may have great endurance and patience (NIV).

We have the opportunity to live fully and totally in our true identity. God is willing to fill us with knowledge, wisdom, and understanding through the Spirit. With Him, we are able to live a worthwhile life and do good works in the strength of Jesus.

Praise God for the characteristics He has placed into your identity. Use the verses above to write a personal prayer.

_____
_____
_____
_____

Week Four - The Strategies of the Thief

Some victims try for years to undo the damage of identity theft. Identify theft disrupts your life. Functioning in a usual way is paralyzed. Identity theft maligns your name. It robs you financially. It destroys your reputation, denies your rights, and expends much energy. We have a friend whose identity was stolen. He was unaware until he tried to board an airplane; he was stopped at the security line and asked several questions. His name had been used fraudulently and now he was on a watch list at the airport. He contacted several government offices to obtain an identity clearance. It took months. Every time he went to the airport, he had to arrive hours in advance and endure a lengthy process before being allowed to board the aircraft. It was time-consuming and costly.

There is another kind of identity theft, even more costly and devastating. It has eternal consequences. It is spiritual, and it affects all segments of our lives. In this kind of identity theft, we know the name and character of the thief. He seeks to steal our God-given identity.

Read John 8:44:

> He was a murderer from the beginning, not holding to the truth, for there is no truth in him. When he lies, he speaks his native language, for he is a liar and the father of lies (NIV).

In the verse, Jesus is referring to Satan. How does Jesus describe him?

_____

_____

_____

Jesus called him the father of lies and deceitful in all things. Nothing would please Satan more than to cause you or me to squander our identity in Christ.

According to Revelation 20:10, Satan is the master deceiver. Through deception, he robs us of our God-given identity.

Read John 10:10a:

> The thief comes only to steal and kill and destroy.

Define the word "thief."

_____
_____
_____

According to John 10:10a, what is the thief's only purpose?

_____
_____

Satan wants to destroy your identity. If we lose sight of our God-given identity, we will not be able to fully live as Jesus promised: "I have come that they may have life and that they may have it more abundantly" (John 10:10b NKJV). Most of us haven't lived totally in the fullness of all that Jesus has planned because the enemy has stolen from us.

Throughout life—regardless of our age, occupation, or background—the enemy attacks our identity. He never goes on vacation.

Image distortion and identify theft are part of the strategic plan of our enemy. His is a well-thought-out scheme. He knows our weaknesses and vulnerabilities. He will flaunt our flaws and limitations until we question his strategy and combat it. Recognizing the deception isn't always easy, but Paul tells us how to go into combat.

Week Four
Day One
He Robs

"Have you seen my wallet?" My husband Duncan asked as he walked into the kitchen. He was dressed for work but perplexed because his wallet was missing.

"No, I haven't seen it." I began looking around the room. "When was the last time you remember having it?"

"Oh, no," he sighed. "I must have left it on the bumper of the car last night when I bought gas." He reached for the phone to call the credit card company.

Within the ten short hours since driving away from the gas station, Duncan's credit card had been used to make purchases, open new accounts, and order tires for a truck he didn't own. One merchant said, "You don't sound like the Duncan who just opened these accounts."

His identity had been stolen.

According to Javelin Strategy and Research, more than ten million U.S. citizens are victims of identity theft each year, and more than thirty-five million data records are compromised in corporate and government security breaches. Experts estimate businesses around the world have lost more than $221 billion a year due to identity theft. False identity is a common, pervasive, and growing problem.

False is the key word. False identity is deceitful and does not look, act, or sound the same as the real thing. False identity is dishonest because the intent is to use your good name to cheat a merchant or service provider. A thief steals your worthy name because his or her own name or reputation or credit worthiness is defective.

Have you seen the commercial where two sweet-looking elderly ladies, Thelma and Betty, are sitting on a couch next to each other daintily sipping coffee? When they begin to speak, you expect to hear two sweet little voices. Instead you hear the voices of two loud, raucous, red-neck men, laughing and teasing about the awesome Harleys they just rented for free—courtesy of Thelma and Betty's credit cards. Funny commercial. Not so funny situation. That's identity theft.

Identity thieves assume your personal identity, do things you would never do, say things you would never say, and buy things you would never purchase. The thief pretends to be you.

How do you recognize if you have been the victim of spiritual identity theft? We can only recognize fake identity by studying what the original looks like.

Read Galatians 5:22-23:

> But the fruit of the Spirit is love, joy, peace, patience, kindness, goodness, faithfulness, gentleness and self-control. Against such things, there is no law (NIV).

According to this verse, what are the results of living in the Spirit?

_____
_____
_____
_____

When we fall prey to the robber, we no longer walk in the benefits of our true identity – love, joy, peace, patience, kindness, goodness, faithfulness, gentleness, self-control. Instead, unforgiveness, bitterness, resentment, and fear invade our lives. We become captives who are unable to freely love, freely serve, freely give, and freely forgive. We act out of insecurity and fear as we try to prove who we are. When he steals from us, we will start behaving, sounding, and acting in ways that are not consistent with our God-given identity.

Read Ephesians 6:10-13:

> Finally, be strong in the Lord and in his mighty power. Put on the full armor of God, so that you can take your stand against the devil's schemes. For our struggle is not against flesh and blood, but against the rulers, against the authorities, against the powers of this dark world and against the spiritual forces of evil in the heavenly realms. Therefore put

on the full armor of God, so that when the day of evil comes, you may be able to stand your ground, and after you have done everything, to stand.

My friend Renee said it like this. "Umm. God is passing out armor – that should be a clue.xx We are in a battle."

A robber is a cunning, devious person who wants to steal what you have. The robber doesn't want to work for the prize; he would rather take what you've worked for instead. While on vacation, a friend's daughter's wallet was taken. In that wallet was the total savings the girl had accumulated prior to the trip. She had worked at several jobs and saved almost every dollar she made so she would have spending money. After the thieves took the money, she was inconsolable. The thieves took much more than money; they broke her heart.

Thieves find the weakest spot and moment to strike. They love to raid in the dark, undetected. They get in, steal, and get out as fast as possible. A neighbor left his home one morning for a few minutes to pick something up at the hardware store. While he was gone, thieves broke in, smashed lamps and vases, and scattered belongings all over the house. They must have watched him leave and saw their opportunity. They grabbed the jewelry and guns and left as fast as they entered. When the neighbor returned, he discovered the mess the thieves had left.

You enemy will watch your life for the most opportune time to swoop in and do whatever damage he can do to your identity. He will take what is valuable and try to leave undetected, but he will always leave you with the mess to clean up.

Satan attacks, but we are made fit for the battle. We can be aware and prepared for the thief. When we know our identity in Christ we are to stand in that identity and not back down to the lies and deception of our enemy.

Week Four
Day Two
He Lies

The enemy twists the truth. When the serpent deceived Eve, he mixed truth with lies to mislead her. Even though there was some truth in what he said, it became a full-blown lie as he added false statements.

Read Genesis 3:1-5:

> Now the serpent was more crafty than any of the wild animals the LORD God had made. He said to the woman, "Did God really say, 'You must not eat from any tree in the garden'"? The woman said to the serpent, "We may eat fruit from the trees in the garden, but God did say, 'You must not eat fruit from the tree that is in the middle of the garden, and you must not touch it, or you will die.'" "You will not certainly die," the serpent said to the woman. "For God knows that when you eat from it your eyes will be opened, and you will be like God, knowing good and evil" (NIV).

The serpent is identified in Revelation 12:9.

> The great dragon was hurled down—that ancient serpent called the devil, or Satan, who leads the whole world astray. He was hurled to the earth, and his angels with him.

Who is the serpent? _____

In your own words, write what happened in the garden (from the Genesis passage above).

_____
_____
_____
_____
_____

Satan approached Eve, quoting the words of God. He mixed error with truth. He tricked Eve with a lie masquerading as truth. He lied. She was intrigued by the special knowledge she might get from eating the fruit. The serpent said to Eve, "You can be like God!"

The enemy lied to Eve. List as many lies as you can find from the passage above in the space below.

_____
_____
_____
_____

Eve was enticed by the idea she could be like God. If Eve had seen the truth, she would have been able to say no to Satan. She would have known she was created in the image of the Father. Satan implied God was withholding something good from her, something she needed, and that something would make her incomplete.

Her eyes went out of God-focus. God was no longer central. She replaced her divinely-created image with an imagination of something better. She ate the fruit believing it would help her achieve a new, more complete self-made image. Satan lied to Eve by changing what God said, and he has been doing it ever since.

Recall a time when you believed there was something you just had to have. If you didn't receive it you would be incomplete, inadequate, deficient. (For example, a job, a relationship, a new outfit, a facelift, etc.)

_____
_____
_____

Satan is still twisting the truth. Let's take outward appearance as an example.

Read 1 Samuel 16:7

> But the LORD said to Samuel, "Do not consider his appearance or his height, for I have rejected him. The LORD does not look at the things people look at. People look at the outward appearance, but the LORD looks at the heart" (NIV).

God looks at your heart. God says beauty comes from inside. But Satan lures us with airbrushed photos of impossibly tall and thin models and movie stars. We are intrigued and seduced to believe outward appearance is most important. We might be convinced to spend excessive time and money to beautify our appearance. He whispers to us in magazine ads and television commercials, "Being beautiful is all that matters!"

I remember how stocky I was in high school. Twiggy was a famous model. (Anyone remember skinny Twiggy?) But no matter what I did or didn't do, I could never be as thin as Twiggy. I even bought a body suit to wear when exercising. The suit was made of plastic and made me sweat. If I inflated it and put it on, I looked like I was headed for Mars in my space suit. I know it sounds so ridiculous – now – but then, I somehow believed the lie. When I removed that body suit, I was sweaty and worn out, but my figure had not been "magically" transformed. I still did not have the Twiggy figure that I believed I needed.

Don't believe Satan's version of God's truth; read the Word and discover the truth of real beauty. God gave women special elegant, lovely, soft, and gracious attributes to make us beautiful and attractive. There is nothing wrong with using products or services to improve our appearance. The danger comes when we think we need to have those things in order to be complete. Don't misunderstand me. I am all for using every available means to have beautiful skin, hair, and a healthy body, but be sure to keep your heart and life focused on the precious and beautiful relationship with God.

Paul wrote in his letter to the church of Corinth.

> "All things are lawful for me," but not all things are helpful. "All things are lawful for me," but I will not be enslaved by anything (1 Corinthians 6:12 ESV).

What did Paul say was lawful?

_____

Even though he considered all things lawful, what did he say about them?

_____
_____
_____
_____

If we believe the lies of the enemy, we will become desensitized to honesty. This numbness triggers our human nature's natural tendency to dishonesty. We may exaggerate or embellish the truth. If we aren't aware of the enemy's lies, we can become liars too.

Before the day is over, set aside some time to reflect on the lies of the enemy. Ask yourself if you have become his victim by believing his lies. Then think through your conversations over the past week (yes, emails and social media count). Have you amplified or inflated the truth to make yourself look good? Have you stretched the truth? Have you added to the story to make it better?

Write your thoughts in the space below.

_____
_____
_____
_____
_____
_____

Satan is a liar. He will take your identity from you by changing the truth about your identity.

Week Four
Day Three
He Misrepresents

The enemy distorts our view and misrepresents God and all things righteous. In our passage yesterday, notice how Satan turned Eve's focus toward herself. He said, "…your eyes will be opened…and you will be like God…." (Genesis 3:5).

Instead of focusing on the truth God had said or the beautiful things she already had, the enemy caused Eve to wonder what she was missing. Her attention was averted from God to self.

What are the enticements in your life that divert your attention from God?

_____
_____
_____
_____

The enemy is still deceiving us with these words. He whispers, "You are all that matters."

If my focus becomes all about me, I might start to think God is concealing something from me because I can't have what I want, my way, in my timing, the way I want it. I can be manipulated into thinking God is withholding from me. How many times have I fallen into this same trap? As if my Creator, my Maker, my Friend, the Savior of my soul, the One who crafted and formed and fashioned me and who loves me completely, and accepts me unconditionally, is withholding something good from me.

God does withhold things from us sometimes, but not the things He knows will benefit us and are helpful. He loves us and gives everything needed to equip us to live according to our full image-bearing potential. Satan tries to direct our focus away from the goodness of God.

The psalmist wrote, "No good thing does He withhold from those who walk uprightly" (Psalm 84:11 ESV).

Have you ever believed God was withholding something good from you?

___

Read Psalm 31:19:

> How great is your goodness, which you have stored up for those who fear you, which you bestow in the sight of men on those who take refuge in you (NIV).

What promise are we given in this verse?

___

Once, during a very busy and hectic season of our lives, this verse made a huge impact on my life. Our three daughters were in the stage of life where they had all sorts of extracurricular activities.

We were trying to sell our home and no one was buying. It had been more than two years! When we finally received a contract, we closed the deal fast—before we found a new house. So our family of five along with our big black Labrador retriever moved into a rental townhouse. We thought we would live there for a month or two.

Living out of boxes worked okay at the beginning, but one month turned into two, and two into three, three into four, and four into five. The townhome had little space for entertaining or for the girls to host sleepovers. And the box clutter made it anything but tidy. How was I supposed to make this new place a home? Was I a failure as a homemaker? In about the sixth month, I remember driving down the street asking God, "What's the deal? Is there something we aren't doing right? Why is this taking so long?"

The quiet answer I heard in my spirit was this phrase from Psalms, *No good thing does He withhold...* (Psalm 84:11). And the right view occurred to me. If owning another property to live in at that time was a "good thing" for our family, then God would not be withholding it.

In my heart, I realized my role as a homeowner and homemaker had become tied to my identity. That day, I quit stressing about the house situation. I really did. We made the most out of living out of boxes and actually began to appreciate the simplicity of fewer things. We continued to look for a new home, but the anxiety and pressure of finding a place was gone. Sounds like such an easy concept, doesn't it? But sometimes we cannot grasp the truth.

Even though my role may have changed, my identity had not. Cramped, cluttered, and all, God was actively working in and through me.

Months later, when we located a home, it turned out to be a wonderful time of celebration for our family. We surprised our daughters on Christmas morning by driving to our new home. That Christmas gift has been a much-talked-about family memory.

We learned more from the experience, too. We learned patience; we learned the freedom of simplicity; we learned how to trust; and we learned the promises of God come through faith and patience (see Hebrews 6:12).

Describe a challenging time in your life when you doubted God.

_____

_____

As you think of this difficult time, consider the progression of our enemy's strategy. The fundamental purpose of the enemy is to destroy. He never tells us he is going to destroy us, but he subtly tries to cause us to doubt the truth and the God of truth.

He tempts us to believe his way is better. The enemy portrays sin as easy, fun, and necessary.

Read 2 Corinthians 11:14:

> Satan himself masquerades as an angel of light.

How does Paul describe Satan?

_____

_____

What does the word "masquerade" mean?

_____
_____
_____

Satan is the master magician. He pretends he is the bearer of fun, excitement, and beauty—light. He changes dark into light, and if we fall into his dark pit, our true identity as a child of God is stolen.

Satan has the world at his disposal to convince us that darkness is light

He makes it easy for us to choose the wrong path. He entices us to give in to sin, insinuating that it's not a big deal. Later we find out how costly it is.

Since Satan is a masquerader, we need to be on the lookout for his disguises. He disguises himself as a teacher, but he is a false teacher. He is industrious, promotes error, and undermines the truth.

A few years ago our daughter purchased flowers for a friend using an Internet flower service. As she was placing her purchase, she checked the boxes on the order form that appeared to be necessary for an easy and fast completion of her transaction.

The flowers were delivered and the appropriate amount charged to her account. Later, when she carefully reviewed her bank statement, she came across a recurring charge for $14.95. She noticed the charges appeared every month since the purchase of those flowers. Those withdrawals eventually added up to almost $200.

When she researched the flower company name online, she discovered others had also been scammed. The box that appeared to be necessary for completing her order in an easy and convenient way was actually an authorization for a monthly fee. It was voluntary but appeared to be necessary. The company tricked thousands of customers with fine print and a tiny box.

Our true enemy, the one who comes to steal, kill, and destroy in the spiritual realm, has also mastered the fine print. His fine print starts with redirecting our focus from God to ourselves. How easy it is for us to think something is good for us when it isn't.

That huge ice cream sundae with all the toppings is sweet and delicious, but too many will clog your arteries and put inches on your hips. Starving yourself to be thin seems like a good idea, but without the proper nutrients, your health will fail. The most common answer from drug abusers when asked why they use drugs is, "It makes me feel so good." Yet those same drugs will drag a person into a pit of despair. A married man gets involved in an adulterous affair because "it feels so right."

Satan is full of the raw, dirty, evil things of this world—darkness.

We believe the enemy's enticing claims to happiness even though the choices are outside of God's way. We desire the possessions and positions he dangles in front of us. He offers us a quick "check box" to instant gratification. His quick pleasures are never completely satisfying and we find ourselves in a place of confusion and delusion and captivity. And like the mounting costs of the monthly fees from the flower company, his schemes cost us more than we can imagine. Painful consequences follow choices based on Satan's schemes and lies.

Satan's ultimate goal is for us to be disillusioned with God and give up living in God's plan. He will use anything and anyone to tempt us to quit.

One of his most effective methods is using our failures and sins to defeat us.

Week Four
Day Four
He Accuses

The enemy says we are disqualified and throws accusations into our path. He will blame you for ruined relationships and point his bony finger at you when you make mistakes.

Read Revelation 12:9-10:

> So the great dragon was cast out, that serpent of old, called the Devil and Satan, who deceives the whole world; he was cast to the earth, and his angels were cast out with him. Then I heard a loud voice saying in heaven, "Now salvation, and strength, and the kingdom of our God, and the power of His Christ have come, for the accuser of our brethren, who accused them before our God day and night, has been cast down (NKJV).

Answer the following questions.

Who is the accuser?

_____

_____

Whom does he accuse?

_____

_____

When does he accuse?

_____

_____

Satan not only deceives, he accuses. Day and night Satan accuses "the brethren." Relentless accusation. Have you ever awakened in the middle of the night to his accusations? Perhaps right in the middle of your day you hear his condemning voice. Has Satan ever accused you with statements like these? Put a check by the ones he has whispered in your ear.

- ☐ You're messed up again; you're a liability to God.
- ☐ You are so selfish; you are never going to change.
- ☐ Why bother to draw near to God? You'll just wander away again, anyway.
- ☐ After what you just did, do you really believe God still accepts you?

When we make a mistake or say the wrong thing or even rebel, our enemy tells us we are disqualified to be a true woman of God. He pushes us to a point where we will never try again. He would love to see us on a shelf never attempting anything godly again. Nothing would please Satan more than for us to be complacent and apathetic.

Because we still live in our fleshly bodies, we do wrong things. We say hurtful words or struggle with forgiveness and bad feelings toward others. We spend too much or eat too much. We stretch the truth to make ourselves look good. Our sinful actions, words, and attitudes grieve the Lord, but our status as a beloved child never changes. God is willing to forgive us and He guides us back to the right path, but along the way, the enemy holds up a disqualified sign. The enemy comes to us with thoughts like, "You are not created in God's image." Or he plants questions into our minds. "Created by God? Are you are kidding me? Fearfully and wonderfully made? Are you crazy?"

He wants us to abandon our dream and relinquish our place in God's service. We must never ignore our own sin, but we can't let it cripple us either.

In the space below write about a time when you wanted to give up. What were some of the reasons for you wanting to quit? Did you feel disqualified or clumsy or inept or hopeless?

_____
_____
_____
_____

Regardless of our actions, he accuses us. Have you ever found that you hear His accusing voice, especially when you are about to pray or share your faith or serve God in some way?

I heard about a woman who started a Bible group for pre-teen girls. On the first day only one girl attended the meetings. Every week, others were invited but none came except the one girl. I might have been discouraged enough to stop, but this lady kept on. She prepared for that one little girl as if she was preparing for hundreds. When regional or statewide meetings were held and other churches brought large groups of girls, the woman attended with the one girl.

Satan accuses. He whispers, "You failed and you messed up." But this woman didn't listen to the voice of her accuser. She never gave up. She didn't succumb to his accusations. I've often wondered about the impact she had on the life of one pre-teen girl. The key to winning over the accuser is to learn to recognize the enemy's voice. He will not identify himself, but he will pull you away from fellowship with God and he will push you toward feeling inadequate.

There is a great difference between the voice of God and the voice of the enemy. Have you ever been in a crowded room and heard the voice of a child crying? The ears of every mother in the room perk up at the first sound of the cry, but one mom will instantly recognize the cry of her own child. She is the one who will respond because she knows the voice of her child. I've even heard a mom say, "Oh, that's just her happy voice; she's not hurt." Not only does the mom know the voice of her child, she knows the nuance of whether the child really needs her or not.

Shepherds have a distinctive call and voice so that the flock knows the voice of the shepherd. In a large group of sheep, several shepherds can make their individual calls and the sheep will separate and gather around the respective shepherd, because the sheep know the voice.

As children of God we can know His voice. We can also learn the voice of the enemy so we won't respond to him.

Imagine what God would say if He spoke to you.

_____
_____
_____

What kinds of words would the enemy say?

_____
_____
_____
_____
_____
_____

Read John 10:27:

>My sheep listen to my voice; I know them, and they follow me (NIV).

Follow the voice of Jesus when the accuser tries to blame and denounce you.

Week Four
Day Five
He Seduces

The enemy entices us to doubt God. His arguments and ideas are seducing to our souls.

Trust is developed in the confines of a relationship. The enemy does not have a relationship with God, so he tries to rob everyone else from having one as well. If Satan is successful in redirecting our focus, he then can redirect our trust. Self-focus leads to trust in self instead of trust in God.

Read Genesis 3:6-10:

> When the woman saw that the fruit of the tree was good for food and pleasing to the eye, and also desirable for gaining wisdom, she took some and ate it. She also gave some to her husband, who was with her, and he ate it. Then the eyes of both of them were opened, and they realized they were naked; so they sewed fig leaves together and made coverings for themselves. Then the man and his wife heard the sound of the LORD God as he was walking in the garden in the cool of the day, and they hid from the LORD God among the trees of the garden. But the LORD God called to the man, "Where are you? He answered, "I heard you in the garden, and I was afraid because I was naked; so I hid (NIV).

Describe Adam and Eve's behavior.

_____
_____
_____
_____

First, they based their decision on a lie. Then, they lied and hid from God. They even hid from one another. Both Adam and Eve covered themselves with leaves to hide their nakedness. The exposure they felt was more than naked bodies; they also feared intimacy and transparency. For the first time they felt shame, a full 180-degree shift in their identity.

Adam and Eve were manipulated by Satan and believed his lies, which caused them to lose trust in the Creator. Lack of trust caused a loss of fellowship. Fellowship with the One who truly loved and cared for them. Fellowship with the One who had given them true identity. Fear invaded their lives.

From the moment they believed and acted on the lie, Adam and Eve became victims of identity theft and began to live in a way not according to their true image.

Unfortunately, we follow the example and pattern of the garden. First, a less-than-the-full-truth thought enters our mind. We mull the thought over and over until we act on it and before we know it, we have been manipulated by the lie into doing something that is not according to our image. Then, we try to cover it up and hide. Sounds so ridiculous to think we can hide from God, but we try. We make excuses and rationalizations. Even though God loves us constantly, we hide from Him thinking we don't deserve to be in His presence.

Have you noticed the progression of the enemy's tactics? First, he manipulates God's words just enough to replace devotion to God with attention to our needs and wants. Then, he turns our attention inward to fixate on ourselves. We no longer look to our Father and trust in Him, His provisions, and His timing. Our desires become our primary focus. The enemy directs our focus to the temporary and then he pushes us to get what we want right now! Instant gratification. Once we act on his lies, he accuses us and questions our God-given identity. We no longer believe we can have fellowship with God.

The pattern is a downward spiral. In your own words, describe a time when you fell prey to Satan's tactics?

_____
_____
_____
_____

The more we go down this path, the less we walk in our true identity.

The good news is we do not have to continue to operate according to Satan's schemes. We have the truth at our disposal. Take time. Seek wise counsel. Read, study, and meditate on the Word of God. See if your decision lines up with the truth. Don't be in a hurry.

If you are in doubt about a choice or a decision or a teaching, ask God for wisdom. "If any of you lacks wisdom, you should ask God, who gives generously to all without finding fault, and it will be given to you" (James 1:5 NIV).

What does this verse promise?

_____
_____

When you pray, believe. God will show you the truth. The devil does not have a varied playbook. He follows the same game plan every time. The same tricks he played on Eve, he tries on you and me. See the schemes and tactics of the enemy. Recognize his tactics. Never let the devil set your agenda.

Let's learn to catch on quicker. Let's take a stand against the enemy by submitting to God and His truth. Let's refuse to be the enemy's victim. Don't hide from God, run to God. It's in His presence we are empowered and equipped to walk in our true identity.

Take a moment and ask God to expose any ways that you have been deceived by the enemy. List the lies you will stop believing.

_____
_____
_____
_____
_____
_____
_____
_____
_____
_____

Use this Scripture as a reference to pray for yourself daily discernment and understanding of your righteousness in Christ Jesus:

> And this is my prayer: that your love may abound more and more in knowledge and depth of insight, so that you may be able to discern what is best and may be pure and blameless for the day of Christ, filled with the fruit of righteousness that comes through Jesus Christ—to the glory and praise of God (Philippians 1:9–11 NIV).

****

GOING DEEPER

The enemy is crouched and ready to steal our identity. He will employ every tool and trick of the trade to accomplish his fiendish goal. He will rob us and try to take all the things we have worked so hard for away from us. He will lie. In fact, he is the father of all lies. His lies won't seem like lies and if we aren't careful, we will believe the wrong things he tells us. He will accuse us and make us believe we are worthless. He will misrepresent God to try to confuse our minds and souls. He will seduce us to want what isn't good for us.

Sometimes our enemy dangles shiny objects over us and tries to convince us that we need them. He may try to convince us that an illicit affair is okay because it feels so right, or that taking money from our job is not too bad since the employer doesn't pay us enough anyway. He may make us think that the harsh words we say are okay because the person deserved it. These are ways he robs our identity from us.

If you had a large butcher knife in your hand, a two-year-old might think it was a beautiful shiny object. The child would beg and cry and plead, but you would never give the child the knife because you know it would be dangerous to the child.

God sometimes doesn't let us have what looks shiny and wonderful because he knows we could be harmed. Instead of believing the lies and enticements of the enemy, trust God to provide everything you need and desire.

Read and memorize the following Scriptures.

1 Timothy 6:17:

> Command those who are rich in this present world not to be arrogant nor to put their hope in wealth, which is so uncertain, but to put their hope in God, who richly provides us with everything for our enjoyment (NIV).

Psalm 107:9:

> For he satisfies the thirsty and fills the hungry with good things (NIV).

Hebrews 13:21:

> [He will] equip you with everything good for doing his will, and may he work in us what is pleasing to him, through Jesus Christ, to whom be glory for ever and ever. Amen (NIV).

Week Five - Defeat the Thief

In Week One, we discussed how we frequently don't choose truths from the Bible when describing ourselves. When we have accepted or believed other sources that don't line up with the Bible, we have allowed lies to be tattooed on our minds. One pastor said, "I can't afford to have a thought in my head that is not in God's head about me."[xxi]

Believing the wrong thing is a common temptation. I have been working hard to believe my own true identity. Even after I became a Christian, I thought I had to earn God's approval. I have spent almost thirty years in the ministry and it is humbling to say I still struggle with confidently and securely knowing my true identity in Christ. I still succumb to the lies of the enemy. The lies are all around us every day. It's easy to say the right things, but firmly grasping the truth requires us to set our minds on the truth and replace the lies. Living in truth is a constant battle. We are continually bombarded with words, circumstances, and experiences that are contrary to the truth of true identity.

When we describe ourselves with false identity labels, we give the enemy victory. In the list below, circle the words that you sometimes believe about yourself.

FALSE IDENTITY

Left out

Outcast

Empty

Alone

Bored

Forgotten

If you are like most people, you have circled at least one in the false identity category. Remember we identified our thief as Satan, the father of lies. His lies are potent, forceful, and influential. Potent words hurt; they wound and lead to error.

The next time you feel defeated, focus on the words and Scriptures of true identity listed below. Potent lies are made impotent by the truth of God's Word.

TRUE IDENTITY

Chosen (Colossians 3:12)

Adopted, accepted (1 John 3:1-2, Romans 8:15)

Full (1 Corinthians 3:16, Ephesians 2:10)

Never alone (1 Corinthians 6:17, Ephesians 2:18)

Called (John 14:12)

Heir (Romans 8:17)

So let's get started. This week we will see how our true identity words will defeat our enemy the thief.

Week Five
Day One
Chosen and Accepted

Mother Teresa said, "Loneliness and the feeling of being unwanted is the most terrible poverty." Imagine a child on the playground as the captains choose teams. The child is chosen last because he or she isn't the best at the game, so the same child grows up believing he or she will never be good at sports. Being left out feels terrible, and the feeling can follow into adulthood. Then the feelings expand from sports to everything. All of us have been left out at one time or another. We know what it feels like. If we base our identity on an incident or a number of incidents, the negative impact will affect our willingness and ability to grasp what God has planned for us. We will shrink back in intimidation.

Describe a time when you felt left out.

_____
_____
_____
_____
_____
_____
_____

Read Colossians 3:12:

> But God said, "Therefore, as God's chosen people, holy and dearly loved, clothe yourselves with compassion, kindness, humility, gentleness and patience" (NIV).

Now read 1 Peter 2:9:

> But you are a chosen people, a royal priesthood, a holy nation, God's special possession, that you may declare the praises of him who called you out of darkness into his wonderful light (NIV).

God chose you because He loves you and He knows you are worthy. We are not left out by God but chosen. We will never live out our true identity in Christ if we do not believe we have been chosen. Others may have left us out, but God has not.

Reread the two verses above again. Describe the attributes and actions of "chosen" people.

_____
_____
_____

We should live each moment of each day as a reflection of our chosen identity. If you determine to be compassionate, kind, humble, gentle, and patient, you will mirror the image of God. Begin by praising God in all situations. Instead of complaining about dishes to wash, thank God for the plates and saucers and the food to serve your family. Rather than grumble about not having the latest shoe style, praise God for feet and the ability to walk. He has chosen you to be His child. He loves you with unconditional love. Live in your chosen-ness.

If not, you are operating under false identity. Reject that "left out" identity. Declare today that God has chosen you. And because He has chosen you He has equipped you to walk in your true identity.

When I am unkind, impatient, arrogant, etc., I realize I have stepped into false identity. I ask the Holy Spirit to reveal to me what lie I have believed. I want to consistently walk in my true identity in Christ.

Our society is built around feeling accepted and approved. Peer pressure to be accepted can lead us down wrong paths. We all want to feel loved and accepted. Studies indicate that the reason kids join gangs is because they want to belong to a group. Peer pressure is found in every age group, every socio-economic background, and every phase of life. Many times the paths we choose may not be "bad" but the only reason we are choosing it is to avoid rejection. No one likes rejection.

What factors might make a child feel rejected?

_____
_____
_____

What factors might make an adult feel rejected?

_____
_____
_____
_____
_____

Everyone experiences rejection. The wounds of rejection are deep because they are so negative and dismissive and because rejection attacks our identity.

Rejection hurts, but acceptance is a powerful motivator. Our dear friend Chase is in her twenties and is a beautiful, athletic, intelligent, fun Christian woman. But Chase suffered from rejection. Her negative feelings stem from the fact that she is adopted. Her adopted parents are loving, kind, generous, giving parents. They love Chase. Throughout her life, they have told her how much they wanted her as their daughter and assured her of the great love they have for her. But some inner emotions and senses and conflicts prevented Chase from receiving their love.

As a baby, Chase never allowed her mom or dad to rock her to sleep or to comfort her when she was hurt or even to tuck her into bed. In the third grade, she became irritable, unruly, and disobedient to her teachers. One night she ordered her mother out of her room and screamed, "Find me my real mother!" Knowing she was adopted had created a wall of rejection in her heart. She thought, *If I could only find my birth mother, everything will be okay.*

Chase's parents prayed constantly and loved her through all the difficulties. One day, Chase came out of her room and said, "Mom, I know you and Dad love me. I know it, but I cannot feel it."

Chase's mom answered, "Chase, darling, I'm trying to understand your pain but most of all, I am praying for you every day. I want you to know that God is bigger than all your feelings and pain."

Finally, Chase realized that feelings were not necessarily truth. She decided to believe the truth instead of what she felt. Gradually her feelings changed and she felt accepted and loved by her parents. Today, Chase says she not only knows her parents love and accept her but she also knows God does, too.[xxii]

The Bible explains what being accepted by God means.

Read 1 John 3:1a:

> See what great love the Father has lavished on us, that we should be called children of God! (NIV).

What does God call us?

_____

God accepts us fully and adopts us into His family. Our acceptance is so complete, He asks us to call Him Father.

Read Romans 8:15:

> The Spirit you received does not make you slaves, so that you live in fear again; rather, the Spirit you received brought about your adoption to sonship. And by Him we cry, "Abba, Father" (NIV).

What does the Spirit testify about?

_____
_____
_____
_____

The Spirit Himself testifies with our spirit that we are God's children. No matter how excluded you may feel on earth, your heavenly Father accepts you. Live in acceptance. Don't allow the dismissal of people to intimidate you. Man's words and actions do no dictate, validate, or substantiate who you are. The key to overcoming rejection is to solve identity issues. When we base our identity on the Word of God, we can become immune to the wounds of rejection. You will never fully settle rejection issues until you are convinced that you are accepted, loved, and approved by God. Anyone who believes in Jesus will never be rejected by the Father. He is the source of your true identity. Believe in Him, love Him, and desire His will.

Week Five
Day Two
Full Life

Because of personal pain and loss and struggles, any one of us could become depressed and empty. Daily living is so ordinary and it seems we do the same thing over and over again each day. We can become tired and bored in life. Living in your true identity means defeating the enemy in the areas of contentment and fulfillment. Living in your true identity is a satisfying, gratifying, exciting life. Jesus has more for you than you can imagine.

Read John 10:10b:

> I have come that they may have life and that they may have it more abundantly (NKJV).

What did Jesus promise?

_____

Jesus promised us a full and abundant life.

Read the verses below and then write your response in the space on the next page.

Romans 8:9:

> But you are not controlled by your sinful nature. You are controlled by the Spirit if you have the Spirit of God living in you (NLT).

1 Corinthians 6:19:

> Do you not know that your body is a temple of the Holy Spirit, who is in you, whom you have received from God? You are not your own (NIV).

What makes this full and abundant life possible?

_____
_____
_____

When we accept Jesus as our Lord and Savior, He makes His home on the inside of us. He gives His Spirit to wake us up and fill us with creativity, motivation, and joy. The Bible declares our body is the temple of God. God lives within us. There is nothing dull or shallow about having the Creator of all things living in us and through us.

Your life can be full and rich. Abraham Lincoln said, "And in the end, it's not the years in your life that count. It's the life in your years."

If you feel empty and bored, take a good look at how you are spending your time. Living life to the full requires us to dwell on the Word and focus on the promises of God. He will then fill us with hope and satisfaction.

Read Psalm 16:11:

> Thou wilt show me the path of life: in thy presence is fullness of joy; at thy right hand there are pleasures forevermore (NASV).

Author W. Hay Aitken wrote about the full path of life.

> The man who walks along the path of life lives in the presence of the joy-giving God. Just in so far as he is true to that path of life, and wanders neither to the right hand nor to the left, his joy becomes deeper; nay, he becomes partaker of that very fullness of joy in which God Himself lives, and moves, and has His being. And while such is his experience in the midst of all the trials of life, he has also the privilege of looking forward to grander things yet in store for him, when that higher world shall be reached, and the shadows of time have passed away forever. "At Thy right hand," exclaims the Psalmist, "there are pleasures forevermore."[xxiii]

God wants to give us the fullest life imaginable. We have it available at our fingertips. Reject the lies of the enemy and believe God for a full life.

Read 2 Corinthians 4:7:

> We have this treasure in earthen vessels that the excellence of the power may be of God and not of us (NKJV).

We have a priceless treasure inside of us. The same spirit that raised Christ from the dead dwells in us. Don't lose sight of the treasure God has placed in you. Living full may require trying something new and forcing you out of your comfort zone. Remember, we are made in the image of God. Think about the complexities of His image. Open yourself up to new ideas, new activities; try something different. Don't look back in ten years and say, "Oh, I wish I had tried." Look up and then live out of the abundance of His grace. Ask God and He will show you and enable you to do what He has qualified you to do.

Past heartaches, trials, and tragedies may have changed the plans you had when you were younger and put your dreams on hold. Our mistakes and bad decisions have also played a part in the path we have taken. These negatives don't have to define us, because our true identity is still solid even if we have taken detours. Your dreams can be renewed and realized.

Is there something you have always dreamed of doing but have never told anyone? In the space below, make a list of those dreams.

_____
_____
_____
_____

Read Psalm 37:4-5:

> Delight yourself also in the Lord and He shall give you the desires of your heart. Commit your way to the Lord, Trust also in Him, And He shall bring it to pass.

Consciously commit all your plans to the Lord daily. Delight yourself in His friendship and His love. The fact that you seek your delight in Him will regulate your desires so that you will be inclined to ask only for those things which He willingly desires to grant.

Trusting God for a full life is the quickest way to freedom from identity theft. Living a full life means you can dream and accomplish and set goals and then delight and marvel at the richness of the life God has given you.

Week Five
Day Three
Never Alone

A person who wants to parachute from an airplane begins by belting-up with an expert skydiver and jumping in tandem. The novice experiences all the thrills of the jump but is guided and kept safe by the professional skydiver. When we put our trust and faith in the Lord, we are harnessed to God in the same way.

Read 1 Corinthians 6:17:

> But whoever is united with the Lord is one with him in spirit (NIV).

When we are united with the Lord, what does He promise to us?

_____
_____

And because we have His Spirit, we also have an invitation to spend time with Him.

Read Ephesians 2:18:

> For through him we both have access to the Father by one Spirit.

According to this verse, what does our oneness with Him give us?

_____
_____
_____
_____
_____

With God we are never alone. We are always connected to Him. Even if it feels like we are in the dark and we can't see where to go, the promises of God's Word assure us He is always there

Read Psalm 139:7-12:

> Where can I go from Your Spirit?
> Or where can I flee from Your presence?
> If I ascend into heaven, You are there;
> If I make my bed in hell, behold, You are there.
> If I take the wings of the morning,
> And dwell in the uttermost parts of the sea,
> Even there Your hand shall lead me.
> And Your right hand shall hold me.
> If I say, "Surely the darkness shall fall on me,"
> Even the night shall be light about me;
> Indeed, the darkness shall not hide from You,
> Bur the night shines as the day;
> The darkness and the light are both alike to You (NKJV).

Have you ever asked, "God, where are you?" I have. It seems like God is everywhere, but you can't find Him anywhere.

Describe a time when you felt abandoned by God.

_____
_____
_____
_____
_____
_____

Describe a time when you knew God was near you.

_____
_____
_____
_____
_____

We have to go back to God's Word and be reminded of His promise of continual presence. Rest assured, He is there. You may not feel His tangible presence, but don't rely on those fickle feelings. Start today to trust and rely on the truth of His Word. Put yourself in a position to hear Him. Read your Bible every day. Regularly attend church. Worship Him. Pray. Praise. Ask Him to reveal His presence to you.

My husband and I were facing a significant transition. The decisions before us were life-changing and difficult. We asked God for direction. It seemed He didn't answer. We asked, "God, where are you?" But we heard nothing nor sensed His presence.

At one point, we began to list all the pros and cons and we thought we had found a solution. But we knew we weren't depending on God and we were drawing from our own knowledge and leaning into our human understanding. Even though we could have made our decision based on the facts and our experience, we weren't comfortable because we didn't sense God's guidance.

We asked some friends to join us in prayer. It was a prayer meeting I'll never forget. God's presence and power were evident in the prayers of our friends. Someone quoted a not-so-familiar verse from Isaiah 43:18-19. Then a week later, in a church meeting, the speaker stopped before her presentation. She said, "Before I start teaching tonight, I would like to quote a verse. I think someone might benefit from it." She quoted the same verses from Isaiah 43.

Less than a week later, my husband had a phone conversation with a man from another part of the country. He said, "Duncan, I have a verse for you. It's Isaiah 43:18-19."

Three times in less than two weeks those verses were spoken to us. Was it a coincidence? Absolutely not! God orchestrated it so we would be assured of His constant care and love for us.

The verses gave us direction for our decisions.

> Forget the former things; do not dwell on the past. See, I am doing a new thing! Now it springs up; do you not perceive it? I am making a way in the wilderness and streams in the wasteland (NIV).

Prayer and godly counsel changed everything. I believe God was assuring us of His presence. He never abandons us or leaves us alone to flounder. He is near.

Is there a verse that gave you assurance or confidence in a tough situation? Write that verse here.

_____
_____
_____
_____
_____
_____

No matter how painful your situation, God hasn't abandoned or forsaken you. Believe the truth; reject the lies. God promised to never leave you or forsake you. Hold on to the assurance of His presence. It's a promise.

When you are feeling alone, it helps to recall the times God has been with you in the past, because remembering reminds you that God is always present. You can have total victory over abandonment and isolation if you will put yourself into a position to hear from God through prayer and godly counsel.

Read and memorize Psalm 139:7-12.

Week Five
Day Four
Called

One of the greatest victories we have over the thief is the opportunity to live out the life God has destined for us. God has a purpose and a plan for you. His plan is bigger than we could dream or imagine.

As Christ followers, we should want to live out the life God has destined for us.

Read Acts 13:36:

> For when David had served God's purpose in his own generation, he fell asleep; he was buried with his fathers and his body decayed (NIV).

David served the purposes of God in his own generation. I can't think of anything more fulfilling than to be known as someone who served the purpose of God in my generation.

The enemy is an identity thief, and nothing would please him more than to make you struggle in the arena of purpose. He wants you think it is too late or that because of your past mistakes and calamities, you have no future. He will win if you give up because you think you have missed God's purpose or plan for your life.

However, the enemy is a defeated foe. He does not have the last say in your life. God has a special purpose and destiny for you. Even if your circumstances look dismal and bleak, God will rescue you and your identity. You are called, and if you intentionally live in His will, you will never lose the calling.

Read John 14:12:

> [Jesus said,] Very truly I tell you, whoever believes in me will do the works I have been doing, and they will do even greater things than these, because I am going to the Father.

What does this verse promise?

_____
_____

In his book "The Purpose Driven Life," author Rick Warren states, "The purpose of your life is far greater than your own personal fulfillment, your peace of mind, or even your happiness. It's far greater than your family, your career, or even your wildest dreams and ambitions. If you want to know why you were placed on this planet, you must begin with God. You were born by his purpose and for his purpose. There is a God who made you for a reason and your life has profound meaning."[xxiv]

Start your day with God. His presence will build you up, strengthen you, and give you anticipation and expectation to fulfill the calling.

Read Ephesians 2:10:

> For we are God's [own] handiwork (His workmanship) recreated in Christ Jesus [born anew] that we may do those good works which God predestined (planned beforehand) for us [taking paths which He prepared ahead of time] that we should walk in them [living the life which He prearranged and made ready for us to live] (AMP).

When we are recreated in Christ Jesus, what is planned for us?

_____
_____

You have pre-planned works to accomplish while you are here on this earth. Imagine the possibilities. You have a calling that has nothing to do with fate or luck. Your calling is from God because you are His child. Discovering the call of God is the beginning of the greatest adventure. Nothing is more fulfilling than being ready for the work God has called us to do. God puts the desire in us.

Do you believe God has plans for you? List some of those plans below.

_____
_____
_____

What are some unique gifts you have that will enable you to achieve those plans?

_____
_____
_____
_____

In the space below, describe the work that you believe God has uniquely created you to achieve.

_____
_____
_____

What talents has He given you to help you complete your calling?

_____
_____
_____
_____

Your efforts will be satisfying because you will be using your unique skills, gifts, and talents. God has much more planned for you than you've dreamed possible. We make a choice every waking moment of our lives. When we awaken in the morning, we choose the attitude that will ultimately guide our thoughts and actions through the day. I'm convinced our best attitudes emerge out of a clear understanding of our own identity, a clear sense of our divine mission, and a deep sense of God's purpose for our lives.[xxv]

There is great purpose even in the ordinary days of life. Don't get me wrong. Every task of every day may not be satisfying, but we can grasp the reality of our identity and perform even a menial task knowing there is a larger purpose. No matter what you are experiencing today, stay focused on your identity in Christ and His plans and purposes for your life. I was not created to find a purpose. I was created because God has purpose for me.

When I was raising our three daughters, my mission, as a mother, was to train myself out of a job. My goal was to see our three grown daughters as I do now—thriving as young women who love the Lord; who seek His will; who live as capable, productive, and influential women. The result is wonderful, but along the path, at each stage of their development, I had tasks that were not as satisfying. Let's face it, some days of making lunches, driving carpool, and then arriving home only to get a phone call that a paper or notebook had been left behind are not fun. Add doing laundry; cleaning the house; cooking; doing hours of homework (I've already been in the sixth grade, thank you!); dispensing out discipline; working through hurts and disappointments; dealing with meltdowns about dresses, shoes, and hair styles, and a mom could go crazy. I knew the preordained time for me to raise these girls was prepared by God, and I learned to embrace even the less satisfying moments knowing what God had prepared for me. I am still learning this concept.

What are some routine tasks that might discourage you?

_____
_____

Read Habakkuk 2:2:

> And the LORD answered me: "Write the vision; make it plain on tablets, so he may run who reads it" (ESV).

When discouraged or bogged down in the routine of life, what does the Habakkuk verse instruct us to do?

_____
_____
_____

One concrete step you can take to help you win victory over the thief in the area of your calling is to write a mission statement and a list of life-goals that reflect your vision and purpose. Make it clear and precise. Begin writing it here.

_____
_____
_____
_____
_____
_____

After it is written, refer to it often; keep it in a handy place where you can read it. Refer to it when the ordinary and routine tasks seem tiresome. Keeping the written record of your calling in front of you will help you gain perspective and give you daily victory over the thief.

Week Five
Day Five
Beneficiary

Being a child of God means we have an inheritance. Living in my true identity and reminding myself of how utterly defeated the thief is makes me the beneficiary of all the goodness and power of God. As a beneficiary, I receive all the benefits of the victory, which Jesus has won over the enemy. As a beneficiary, my identity is secure.

Read Romans 8:17:

> Now if we are children, then we are heirs—heirs of God and co-heirs with Christ, if indeed we share in his sufferings in order that we may also share in his glory (NIV).

What does this verse promise regarding our inheritance?

_____
_____
_____

Jesus told the story of a son who took his inheritance and went away from his family to a country far away. He squandered the money on a life of parties and extravagances. Meanwhile, the family at home lost all contact with the young man and feared he might be dead. Finally, the young man came to his senses and went home. The father exclaimed, "'For this son of mine was dead and is alive again; he was lost and is found.' So they began to celebrate" (Luke 15:24 NIV).

We are never the forgotten child; we are part of the family. God never gives up on us no matter how much identity we have lost. You can receive the inheritance God intends you to have. Don't be deceived. Even if you have wandered away from God, you are not forgotten. He is waiting to celebrate your return. He is ready to give you a full and complete life because you are His child.

Our Father is King. We are part of the royal family with all the privileges and honors associated with the imperial line.

God has gifted us with an extraordinary legacy because we are His children. Come to the Father and allow Him to give you your inheritance.

Our inheritance is a future event because we are part of the kingdom of God, but there is also a present tense component of our inheritance. Whenever there is difficulty in life, only the child of God who lives in her true identity can find meaning and purpose and even joy in the worst situations. Our victory over the enemy is even greater because our benefactor is Almighty God.

Read John 16:33:

> I have told you all this so that you may have peace in me. Here on earth you will have many trials and sorrows. But take heart, because I have overcome the world (NLT).

When we have troubles and difficulties, what did Jesus say do and why?

_____

_____

_____

Jesus told us to take heart. In other words, don't worry and don't be filled with anxiety because of misfortunes, problems, dilemmas, or dangers. Jesus has defeated and overthrown the enemy. We don't have to wait for the small battles to be decided because Jesus has won the war. And the win was a rout against the thief who tried to steal our identity. We can know who we are in Jesus and live in the certainty of our inheritance. Jesus is the great victor because he experienced every possible temptation or trial we face.

Read Hebrews 2:18:

> Since he himself has gone through suffering and testing, he is able to help us when we are being tested.

According to this verse, why is Jesus able to help you?

_____

_____

_____

Just after His baptism, Jesus spent time in the wilderness and the enemy met him there. The enemy was determined to steal Jesus' identity. Imagine. Jesus' baptism was the first time anyone recognized Him for who He was. John the Baptist said, "Behold the Lamb," and then God acknowledged Him as the true Son of God by the voice of affirmation, "This is my Son in whom I am well pleased." Then the Holy Spirit anointed Jesus by descending on Him like a dove.

From this high-point moment, Jesus fasted and prayed for forty days in the desert. When he was hungry and tired and weak, the enemy tried to steal His identity.

First the enemy tempted Him with pleasure, then with power, and then with greed. These are the same tools Satan uses against you and me.

Jesus was hungry and the enemy said, "Eat." Jesus said that fasting and being in the presence of God was more important than food. Yet how many times have I given in to satisfying my desires rather than chasing after God.

The thief offered Jesus power by saying if Jesus jumped, angels would rescue Him. The enemy uses this same tactic against us when we believe the lie that we can do anything without Christ. And then the enemy offered the world to Jesus on a silver platter.

> Next the devil took him to the peak of a very high mountain and showed him all the kingdoms of the world and their glory. "I will give it all to you," he said, "if you will kneel down and worship me" (Matthew 4:8-9 NLT).

Physically, the lack of food and water weakened Jesus. The thief took that moment to offer the world to Him. What a farce! Jesus not only owns the world and all the kingdoms in it, He created them. How dare the enemy make such an offer! Yet that's exactly what the enemy does. He tries to get us to crave something we already have.

Never give in to the thief. He wants to destroy you and take away your inheritance. The Word of God will continually give you the right view. You are the child of the King of Kings.

****
GOING DEEPER

Victory over the enemy's lies and destruction brings peace. Defeating the enemy is peace multiplied over and over until it becomes fulfillment. God's triumph over the enemy through us and through the resurrection of our identity allows us to dream big and live life as if we never imagined.

Consider the veracity of God's Word when compared to the lies of the enemy. In the back of this workbook, there is a listing of God's truth about your identity. Take some time this week and read the list. Claim your inheritance by using the principle of replacement. Change your mind by replacing lies with truth. Don't stay trapped in the lies of false identity. You can live in great anticipation because you know God desires for you to live in your full identity.

Read Acts 17:28:

> For in him we live and move and have our being. As some of your own poets have said, "We are his offspring" (NIV).

God is our Father; He gives us everything for life. His blessed peace and joy fills each moment of our lives. Even if the enemy has tried to destroy us, He has defeated Satan in every way and He will restore all good things to us.

Read Psalm 62:1:

> Truly my soul finds rest in God; my salvation comes from him (NIV).

Memorize these two verses so you will be reminded how your Father has totally and completely defeated and destroyed the enemy who would steal your identity.

Week Six - Identity's Guard is the Holy Spirit

Last week, we learned the principle of replacement—replacing lies with truth in order to live in our true God-given identity. This week we will learn how the Holy Spirit acts as a guard to help us apply this principle to everyday life. Guard means "to watch over, to protect a treasure, to keep safely from enemy invaders."

Read Proverbs 4:20-23:

> My son, pay attention to what I say; turn your ear to my words. Do not let them out of your sight; keep them within your heart; for they are life to those who find them and health to one's whole body. Above all else, guard your heart, for everything you do flows from it (NIV).

Setting the Holy Spirit as a guard around us begins with paying close attention to the Word of God. Perhaps the most important step we can take to stop identity theft and guard our hearts is to read the Word and allow the Holy Spirit to set up a perimeter around us.

Scripture prescribes the personal life-borders that will protect us. To protect from identity theft, read, study, and learn the Word of God. It is the vehicle that the Holy Spirit uses to protect and guide you.

The Bible writers were inspired by the Holy Spirit, and Scripture has endured thousands of years intact to remind us of the central teachings of the Gospel, to guard us from error, and to enable us to grow into maturity.

The Holy Spirit helps us understand Scripture and causes it to pierce our hearts so that the truth of God will change and protect us.

The Holy Spirit even helps us to pray if we can't find words.

> In the same way, the Spirit helps us in our weakness. We do not know what we ought to pray for, but the Spirit himself intercedes for us through wordless groans (Romans 8:26 NIV).

The Holy Spirit will protect and guard your identity. He will alert you to the lies of the enemy and help you take the path toward true identity. Call on Him to be the guard of your life.

Week Six
Day One
God's CPR

The Holy Spirit is our guard. His work begins with what I call God's CPR.

Medically, CPR stands for cardiopulmonary resuscitation, an emergency procedure in which the heart and lungs are made to work by manually compressing the chest overlying the heart and forcing air into the lungs.

God's CPR is allowing the truth of God's Word to penetrate into your heart. Reading the Word of God must extend beyond head knowledge. If you allow the Word to permeate your thinking and become the belief of your heart, the truth will circulate through your mind and heart like oxygen flows through your body.

What we believe in our heart is essential and critical to living in our full image-bearing potential. This concept of God's CPR came to me one afternoon as I was sitting in a women's Bible study. I listened to the speaker; I heard God's Word. Though I was present in attendance and I participated in the breathing part of CPR, I didn't actually receive God's complete CPR. I could hear God's Word, but I needed to allow my heart to be "pressed." I was breathing in God's Word but not receiving the life-giving CPR.

Read John 14:16-17:

> And I will ask the Father, and he will give you another Advocate, who will never leave you. He is the Holy Spirit, who leads into all truth. The world cannot receive him, because it isn't looking for him and doesn't recognize him. But you know him, because he lives with you now and later will be in you (NLT).

According to this verse, can we recognize the voice of the Holy Spirit?

_____
_____
_____

The answer is yes, because we know Him and because He lives within us. We can be confident of His presence and leading. We can recognize the voice of the Holy Spirit.

The Holy Spirit lives within us. We know Him. He leads us by teaching us the Word, making it clear and plain. When you read the Word, the Holy Spirit uses the words and phrases to guard and protect you. He is our "identity" guard. When we yield to the Holy Spirit, He makes the truth evident.

Read 2 Corinthians 3:18:

> As the Spirit of the Lord works within us, we become more and more like him and reflect his glory even more (paraphrase).

When the Spirit works within us, what happens?

_____
_____
_____
_____

It's the Holy Spirit's job to produce the character of Christ in us. We need the Holy Spirit's help. You cannot produce your God-given identity in your own strength. When we read the Word, the Holy Spirit reveals the truth and application in the verses. When we spend time in meditation, we give the Holy Spirit an opportunity to transform us. He will take us out of false identity tendencies and lead us to the true path of our unique character and to the fullness of who God made us to be. Pay attention to the Holy Spirit. Yield to His promptings. He is life-giving breath to you.

Read James 1:21:

> … humbly accept the word planted in you (NIV).

What does the word "accept" mean?

_____
_____
_____
_____

The Holy Spirit works in you and plants seeds into your mind and soul as you read the Word. For example, when you read about peace, He embeds a desire for calm and quiet. When you breathe the Word in deeply, the desire is satisfied with harmony and order and serenity.

Have you heard the whisper of the Holy Spirit encouraging you to take on some characteristic of Christ? In the space below, write what He has prompted you to consider.

_____
_____
_____
_____

Receive CPR. Quit resisting. Yield to the Holy Spirit. He knows what you need. Have you ever heard a victim needing CPR say, "Hold on, stop compressing my chest; I think I've had enough"?

If the Spirit whispers, "Forgive," and we continue to hold a grudge, or if He prompts us to speak softly yet we use harsh or mean words, we are not getting the full benefits of God's CPR. Our heart is blocked.

On that day in Bible study, I could hear the Word, but I was not receiving it for me. The teacher spoke the Word of God and said, "You have a purpose," but unless I believed it, I could not live in the freedom and joy of acceptance. I had a choice to make. I could continue to take the shallow breaths of lost identity and think wrongly. I could imagine I was in the middle of a mid-life crisis. I could excuse my irritability or edginess or purposelessness. Or I could line up my desires and thoughts with the Word by making the choice to yield to the Holy Spirit's promptings and think thoughts that lined up with the Word of God.

God's Word clearly says that He has a purpose for me. I had to decide that day who I was going to believe - His Word or my thoughts.

Read Romans 8:28:

> We know that all things work together for good to those who love God, who are called according to his purpose (NRSV).

What promise is in this verse?

_____

_____

_____

God has a purpose in all things, in all time, and in all seasons. Though I didn't perceive His purpose, he had one. Even better, the whole plan was for my good. I had a choice to make. It was clear. I could believe God and continue to trust Him, or I could choose to trust my limited perspective.

Read Proverbs 3:5-6:

> Trust in the LORD with all your heart, and do not lean on your own understanding. In all your ways acknowledge him, and he will make straight your paths (ESV).

What three instructions are found in these verses?

_____

_____

_____

What will He do if you acknowledge Him?

_____

_____

I love how The Message paraphrases this verse.

> Trust God from the bottom of your heart; don't try to figure out everything on your own. Listen for God's voice in everything you do, everywhere you go; he's the one who will keep you on track. Don't assume that you know it all.

It is impossible to receive God's CPR when we think we know it all or if we try to figure out solutions to life's problems on our own. Instead, we must trust in God. But trusting is not always comfortable. The compressions of spiritual CPR may be painful because the Holy Spirit uses the right, true, and powerful Word to replace engrained mindsets. Mindsets that may have had years in the making.

Read Hebrews 4:12:

> For the Word that God speaks is alive and full of power [making it active, operative, energizing, and effective]; it is sharper than any two-edged sword, penetrating to the dividing line of the breath of life (soul) and [the immortal] spirit, and of joints and marrow [of the deepest parts of our nature], exposing and sifting and analyzing and judging the very thoughts and purposes of the heart (AMP).

How do these verses describe God's Word?

_____
_____
_____
_____
_____

God's Word has the power to give me CPR. All I have to do is accept the truth and let it flood my whole being all the way to the deepest parts of my heart and mind. When I receive God's CPR, I will find the true meaning of faith and my identity will be secure.

Week Six
Day Two
Conviction

The Bible, the Word of God, is not merely words in a book. It contains words from God and His words are alive and full of power. The Word is active and effective. The Holy Spirit knows my thoughts and intentions. The Word exposes the depths of my mind and heart. This conviction is for my benefit not my destruction.

Conviction is a sense of guilt about something I've said or done. Sometimes conviction is an uneasy feeling as God exposes the thoughts and purposes in my heart. He does not convict to condemn our identity but to complete our identity. Conviction always brings hope with it.

Paul wrote about this hope in Romans 15:4.

> For everything that was written in the past was written to teach us, so that through the endurance taught in the Scriptures and the encouragement they provide we might have hope (NIV).

According to this verse, what gives us hope?

_____
_____
_____

Read Isaiah 55:8-9:

> "For my thoughts are not your thoughts, neither are your ways my ways," declares the Lord. "As the heavens are higher than the earth, so my ways are higher than your ways and my thoughts than your thoughts."

What does Isaiah explain about God's thoughts?

God's thoughts are superior to ours. Our thoughts are very different from the perfect, holy, complete thoughts of the Lord.

My human reaction is almost always the opposite of what the Holy Spirit would want me to do. I might be quick to hold a grudge if someone hurt my feelings and I would try to avoid the person, but the Holy Spirit prompts me to not only forgive but to bless that person.

If I feel rejected and alone, the Holy Spirit convicts those wrong feelings by reminding me that I am God's child and He loves me as a Father. When I'm irritable, He reminds me to be kind, and when I'm edgy and anxious, He helps me calm down and live in peace as I live in my true identity.

> Learning to close the gap between his promptings and conviction and my human reaction is the essential part of Christian growth. As the Holy Spirit presses our heart and squeezes out the wrong thoughts and mindsets, I grow. Spiritual growth is painful because we are undergoing stretching, molding, and refining by the Holy Spirit. Spend time in God's presence and expect the Spirit to transform you into His image. It is one thing to believe in Christ, another thing to believe like Him. The journey toward Christ likeness will inevitably compel us beyond the boundaries of our human nature and so it should be.[xxvi]

Take in the Word of God, and then allow the Spirit to press the truth into your heart. Right thinking and actions will follow.

Read 1 John 2:1:
> My dear children, I write this to you so that you will not sin. But if anybody does sin, we have an advocate with the Father—Jesus Christ, the Righteous One (NIV).

What is an advocate?
_____
_____
_____

An advocate is a defense attorney. When we fail or make mistakes or sin, we have someone arguing our case before the Father.

Who is our advocate?

___

Jesus Christ who loves us and forgives us for all we do defends us because of the power of His blood sacrifice that washed all our sins away.

If you want to be alive and full of power, active, and effective, allow the Holy Spirit to compress and convict your heart. When the spiritual compression of conviction presses our hearts, confession follows. Confession is admission, acknowledgment, and agreement.

Read 1 John 1:9:

> If we confess our sins, he is faithful and just and will forgive our sins and purify us from all unrighteousness (NIV).

What does God promise if we confess our sins?

___

Agreeing and confessing our sin is only half the truth. The next step is to accept forgiveness and cleansing. We behave what we believe. Satan reminds you of all our past sins and failures with continual accusations. Why? Because Satan's goal is to convince us that we are not worthy of God's fellowship. Well, don't argue with a liar. When he condemns you for committing some sin, don't get in a quarrel, simply agree with him, "You're right, I did sin." Then turn your back on the deceiver and declare, "But God has forgiven and cleansed me." Because of His forgiveness and cleansing I can have fellowship with Him.

Read the following passages of Scripture and underline what God does with our sin.

> As far as the east is from the west so far has he removed our transgressions from us (Psalm 103:12 NIV).

> And furthermore, He will "... hurl all our iniquities into the depths of the sea" (Micah 7:19 NIV).

My sins are hidden; they are gone. My iniquities did not fall overboard; God hurled them. He sent my sin forever into the depths of the sea.

No fishing allowed!

He has removed, cast, blotted out, cancelled, and hurled our sins.

Are there some things you need to confess? Write each one here.

_____
_____
_____
_____
_____
_____
_____

I don't know what sins you're carrying, but I do know that the grace and forgiveness of God is available, and you can begin a fresh start. God will forgive you. Confess each sin to the Lord now. Ask for His forgiveness.

Now go back and mark a line through each one. God has blotted it out, cancelled it, and remembers it no more. Thank God for His forgiveness. You are free.

His forgiveness is complete.

Week Six
Day Three
Transformation

Remember our friend Chase? You may feel like she did. Perhaps you are having trouble believing God's truth. For years, Chase heard God's Word. When she was in middle school, she told her mother, "My head can get it, but my heart cannot receive it. It is like you are trying to pour it in but it is not penetrating. It is sliding right past my heart. I feel like my heart is wrapped in Saran Wrap and it cannot receive the truth." But she didn't give up. Her parents didn't either. They continued to pray for her and speak God's truth to her about her identity.

No matter how ingrained a pattern is in our lives, we are not hopeless. We are not stuck in it forever. Our God transforms. He is in the business of changing lives.

One of the best ways to understand transformation is to go back to junior high science and remember the first lessons we learned about metamorphosis. Remember that term? A caterpillar becomes a butterfly. A tadpole becomes a frog. The whole nature, shape, and formation of an animal is changed, and the transformation is amazing. The colorful butterfly which gives such joy as it flits around the flower garden was once a colorless almost shapeless creature until it was changed completely. The same kind of transformation happens to us when we regain our true identity in Christ. The Holy Spirit helps us become all we were meant to be through the transformative power of God.

Living in tandem with God requires us to continue in the CPR process to develop in the image of Him who created us.

Read Colossians 3:10-11:

> You are living a brand new kind of life that is continually learning more and more of what is right and trying constantly to be more and more like Christ who created this new life within you. In this new life one's nationality or race or education or social position is unimportant; such things mean nothing. Whether a person has Christ is what matters, and he is equally available to all (TLB).

According to this passage, what kind of life are we living?

_____
_____
_____

Who created this new life in us?

_____
_____
_____

Because we are made in the image of God, walking in our full image-bearing potential is possible. Nothing disqualifies us.

Is there one thing in your life that you want to be different? List it here.

_____
_____
_____

Author Timothy Keller wrote, "Believing the gospel is how a person first makes a connection to God. It gives us a new relationship with God and a new identity. We must not think, however, that once believing it, the Christian is now finished with the gospel message. A fundamental insight of Martin Luther's was that religion is the default mode of the human heart. Your computer operates automatically in a default mode unless you deliberately tell it to do something else. According to Luther, even after you are converted by the gospel, your heart will go back to operating on other principles unless you deliberately repeatedly set it to gospel mode."[xxvii]

Read Titus 2:11-14:

> For the grace of God has appeared that brings salvation to all people. It teaches us to say "No" to ungodliness and worldly passions, and to live self-controlled, upright and godly lives in this present age, while we wait for the blessed hope—the appearing of the glory of our great God and Savior, Jesus Christ, who gave himself for us to redeem us from all wickedness and to purify for himself a people that are his very own, eager to do what is good (NIV).

What assurances do these verses give us?

_____
_____
_____
_____

Jesus gave himself for us so we would become a people that are Christ's very own, eager to do what is good. That's our true identity. An eager follower of Christ is enabled by God's grace and the power of the Holy Spirit to respond to the Holy Spirit's promptings.

Underline the phrase "enable by God's grace and the power of the Holy Spirit."

No matter how long it has been or how difficult you think it will be, we can respond to the Holy Spirit's promptings. As I was meditating on this concept I thought about the beautiful fountain in our back yard.

When you open the front door to our home, your eyes are immediately drawn through the large back windows. Just outside those windows is our fountain. Sometimes the sun glistens and the fountain seems fresh and alive, but at the same time it's peaceful. The fountain beckons all who enter to admire its beauty.

Because there are also many trees in our back yard, dead leaves fall year-round. No matter the season, some type of leaf is falling into that fountain. When we first moved in, I eagerly removed every leaf every day, not wanting anything to detract from the refreshing flow of the fountain. I guarded the fountain from the debris. However, over time, I was not so eager to remove the debris. One day the water was no longer crystal clear, no longer flowing freely, and no longer attractive and eye catching. Now it was an eyesore. In fact, it even smelled bad. Cleaning it out was possible but took a lot more work and time than if I had been consistent every day.

Oh, yes, the hard work is worth it and I am so glad when the fountain is clean again. Now I try not to let dead stuff pile up in that fountain. I remove the leaves and twigs before decay sets in.

The fountain is in a perfect place in our yard. But the leaves and sticks and other debris are constantly and consistently landing in the fountain.

Despite where we are positioned, even when we are right where we are supposed to be, we must be on guard. Debris is all around us. Floating about in television, music, books, and opinions. Be diligent and consistent. Don't allow dead, unhealthy, unlovely thoughts and ideas to linger in your mind and heart. Be quick to respond by putting your mind on the things of God and the beauty of His Word and love. Be transformed.

Read 1 John 4:4:

> You, dear children, are from God and have overcome them, because the one who is in you is greater than the one who is in the world.

Repeat that verse aloud. Ask the Holy Spirit to give discernment and wisdom. Ask if there are any lies that you have believed. Ask for freedom from Satan's lies. Ask God to help you set limits around you. Ask God to help you put up walls or fences to keep impure thoughts, wrong concepts, stubborn mindsets, mistaken opinions, and unsafe people out of your life. He hears. He answers. He equips. He gives us power to refute the lies of the enemy.

Week Six
Day Four
Protection

Because the Holy Spirit lives within us, we can overcome the lies of the enemy. However, our enemy continually battles us. He tries to keep us trapped in lies and deception by presuming authority over us. But he lost all rights and authority over our life when we accepted Jesus as our Savior. Our Lord defeated Satan at the cross. As believers, we have the ability to refute and defeat his lies and deception.

Satan is a master convincer. He works on us continuously to persuade and influence our actions. One of my friends repeats a rhyme to remind herself of Satan's defeat.

> "Satan is a defeated foe,
> Does he know you know?"[xxviii]

A father and his daughter are driving in the car. The little daughter notices a bee in the car and she cries out to her father, "Daddy, Daddy, the bee, the bee!" She is terrified. She is afraid. Her father reaches out and grabs the bee in his hand even though the bee stings him.

When he releases the bee, she cries, "No, Daddy, don't let him go."

The dad says, "I took the sting. The stinger is gone." Even though the bee may continue to buzz around, it has no power or authority to sting.

Because the father took the sting, the little girl can ride in peace and calm because she believes her father and she is in his presence.

Satan is defeated. He tries to manipulate us with lies and deception and influence our decisions. But he is a defeated foe.

Read James 4:7:

> Submit yourselves, then, to God. Resist the devil, and he will flee from you (NIV).

What must the devil do when we resist him?

_____
_____
_____

When you allow the Holy Spirit to be your guard and protect you from Satan's presumptuous lies, you will live in freedom and victory.

The Holy Spirit is easy to listen to because everything He tells you will line up perfectly with the Word of God. When the Holy Spirit tells you something, believe Him. He uses the Word to prevent wrong thoughts and ideas from entering into your life.

Satan is easy to listen to as well, but we can refute his lies, deceptions, and enticements if we know the Word. He can "buzz" around all he wants, but because we submit to the truth, he has no authority or power.

Read 1 Peter 5:8:

> Stay alert! Watch out for your great enemy, the devil. He prowls around like a roaring lion, looking for someone to devour (NLT).

What does this verse tell us about Satan's activity?

_____
_____

Satan is always looking for an opportune time to attack. Remember our discussion in Week Four, Day One: Satan robs, but the Holy Spirit protects.

What instructions does this verse give us?

_____
_____

Stay alert. Remain focused on the truth. Continue to listen to the promptings of the Holy Spirit and then compare what you hear with the Word. Don't wander from the truth. If something is causing you to feel overpowered, controlled, or mastered, it may be time to consider what is occupying your mind and who or what you are thinking about. If you feel afraid or anxious, then you may have listened to the wrong voice. Use the Word of God to allow the Holy Spirit to protect your heart, mind, and thoughts.

Read Isaiah 26:3:

> You will keep in perfect peace those whose minds are steadfast, because they trust in you (NIV).

Lack of peace and anxious thoughts are a sure sign you have not guarded your heart. There are numerous life situations that can control our thoughts and capture our minds. A problem with a child or a difficulty at work leave us worried and uneasy. Maybe unforgiveness or bitterness or despair creep into your mind regularly. If you give these kinds of negative thoughts control, you will feel defenseless and vulnerable. Do not fear, because the Holy Spirit is your protector. Redirect your attention to God and stay alert.

I saw a unique example of this concept on our never-to-be-forgotten trip to Africa. One day on a photographic safari we saw a pack of gazelles. We were amazed at the little gazelles that all stood in the same direction, alert and at attention. Our guide commented, "When they are alert, their predators the lions or cheetahs will not try to attack them. The predator waits for one of them to be caught off guard." Just as he spoke those words, we noticed a cheetah stalking a gazelle that was isolated and not paying attention. The cheetah's great speed took the gazelle by surprise. The enemy attacked when the gazelle lost focus and concentration.

Don't give up your position. Your position is in Christ. Stand in God's grace. Don't be like that gazelle who wandered away.

My goodness is God's project; my job is to abide in Him. My success is God's plan; my job is to stick near Him. He will guide me and protect me. In fact, He has great plans.

Read Jeremiah 29:11:

> "For I know the plans I have for you," declares the LORD, "plans to prosper you and not to harm you, plans to give you hope and a future" (NIV).

So often we want to see the whole plan, and to know every detail and see the end from the beginning. He only offers us a little light and a little glimpse. We then must trust Him and allow Him to defend and shelter us.

The Holy Spirit is your protector. Your job is to pay attention.

Week Six
Day Five
Freedom

With the Holy Spirit as our guard, living in our true identity brings tremendous freedom to everyday living. First, we experience freedom from anxiety and pain. When the enemy has snatched all or part of our God-given identity, we live in fear about what might happen. Just as someone who has had her personal identity stolen wonders what the thieves will do with the information they have stolen. Will they open new accounts or charge large sums of money? Will she end up being liable for the forged and phony transactions? Will there be repercussions later when she legitimately tries to use her credit to buy a house or car?

In much the same say, spiritual identity theft leaves us wondering. *I wonder if God can ever use me in His service again because the lies of the enemy are so powerful. Will people consider me a fake and a hypocrite because of my mistakes and my record?*

The fear and anxiety are huge, but the Holy Spirit offers me freedom from those doubts and hesitations by the comfort and power of His presence.

> And the Lord will deliver me from every evil work and preserve me for His heavenly kingdom. To Him be glory forever and ever. Amen! (2 Timothy 4:18 NKJV)

Another freedom the Holy Spirit gives us is the freedom to move forward. With His help, we can put all our sins, failures, mistakes, and rebellion behind us and start over. Our God is the God of second chances. He allows us to make a fresh start as if we had never made the mistakes and bad choices of the past.

Read John 8:36:

> So if the Son sets you free, you will be free indeed (NIV).

Describe how free we are in Christ.

Read Galatians 5:1:

> It is for freedom that Christ has set us free. Stand firm, then, and do not let yourselves be burdened again by a yoke of slavery.

According to this verse, how do we keep ourselves from slavery and live in Christ's freedom?

_____
_____
_____
_____

The loss of freedom began way back in the Garden of Eden (see Genesis 3). Jesus has redeemed us from that drastic loss and we can be free again, when we live in our true identity. Stand firm in your identity.

Choosing God gives us freedom we can't find any other place.

Read 2 Corinthians 3:17:

> Now the Lord is the Spirit, and where the Spirit of the Lord is, there is freedom.

What is present when we are near the Spirit of the Lord?

_____

Not only do we have freedom "from" and freedom "to," in our true identity we are granted freedom "for." Freedom for success. Freedom for purpose and a meaningful life. We don't have to settle for second best; we can move forward.

Freedom is the ability to enjoy all of God's gifts.

Read Psalm 24:1:

> The earth is the Lord's, and everything in it, the world, and all who live in it.

God has not only given us identity but He has richly provided everything for life and enjoyment. Delight in Him and give thanks for all His blessings.

Read 2 Peter 1:2-4:

> Grace and peace be multiplied to you in the knowledge of God and of Jesus our Lord, as His divine power has given to us all things that pertain to life and godliness, through the knowledge of Him who called us by glory and virtue, by which have been given to us exceedingly great and precious promises, that through these you may be partakers of the divine nature, having escaped the corruption that is in the world through lust (NKJV).

According to these verses, what has God given us?

_____
_____
_____

Circle the words "divine nature." How would you relate these two words to what you have learned about your true identity?

_____
_____

If we closely examine this divine nature, we understand that true freedom from identity theft is not about getting my way all the time or indulging my whims.

Read Galatians 5:13:

> You, my brothers and sisters, were called to be free. But do not use your freedom to indulge the flesh; rather, serve one another humbly in love (NIV).

What does Paul say we are to do with our freedom?

_____
_____

God warns us about how to use the freedom we attain in Him.

Read 1 Peter 2:16:

> Exercise your freedom by serving God, not by breaking the rules (The Message).

What is the warning?

_____

_____

Freedom is the choice to live for the good of others.

Read Philippians 2:4:

> … not looking to your own interests but each of you to the interests of the others (NIV).

If we live in our true identity, we will not be inwardly focused. Instead, we will care and comfort others. Jesus Christ is our example. He did not seek His own good but that of others. He did everything for the praise and honor of His Father, and never caused anyone to stumble. When we are like Him in what we do, we are free. It is our choice.[xxix]

Living in freedom means living vertically, with our focus upward on Jesus. He is the source of our identity, and He sustains every life detail. Living in freedom also means living horizontally, with our focus on others. Our freedom allows us to love the unlovely and help the needy. Freedom is a result of living in true identity.

I'd like to challenge you to find a way to secretly serve someone. Service in secrecy liberates you in ways nothing else does. Secret service removes all thoughts of what others might think of us and helps us do good for others without our name ever being known. So begin thinking of some way you can help or aid another person without them finding out that you did it. Consider what you could supply or provide in secret. God smiles when you respond by helping others; do it anonymously. True freedom is the result of living for others instead of recognition.

****
GOING DEEPER

The Holy Spirit is part of the Holy Trinity: Father, Son, and Holy Spirit. The Holy Spirit is a person who sees, hears, and speaks. He has knowledge and wisdom. He searches the deepest spiritual truths.

Read 1 Corinthians 2:10:

> These are the things God has revealed to us by his Spirit. The Spirit searches all things, even the deep things of God (NIV).

We learn a lot about the Holy Spirit in the book of Acts. Just before Jesus ascended to heaven, He explained how the Holy Spirit would reveal to the disciples what they needed to know. These disciples were brokenhearted when Jesus died on the cross, and then when He appeared as the resurrected Savior, they had much to learn. The Holy Spirit would indwell them and teach them all they needed to know.

Jesus also described the Holy Spirit as the Comforter, using a word that meant "another of the same kind." In other words, the Holy Spirit is God.

I encourage you to read the rest of the book of Acts. You will see the Holy Spirit in action. He guides, leads, and even assists the disciples on their travels. They followed Him and trusted His guidance. The Holy Spirit is alive and active.

Memorize John 14:16-17:

> And I will ask the Father, and he will give you another Advocate, who will never leave you. He is the Holy Spirit, who leads into all truth. The world cannot receive him, because it isn't looking for him and doesn't recognize him. But you know him, because he lives with you now and later will be in you (NLT).

Acts 1:8:

> But you will receive power when the Holy Spirit comes on you; and you will be my witnesses in Jerusalem, and in all Judea and Samaria, and to the ends of the earth (NIV).

Look for, listen to, and live in the power of the Holy Spirit

He is fully qualified to be the guard of your identity. Breathe in His power through God's CPR. Listen to the conviction He brings to your heart and mind. Allow Him to transform and protect you. Live in the freedom of trusting Him completely.

Week Seven - Flourish in Your True Identity

God's primary purpose for each of us is not about what we do or accomplish. God is much more concerned with what we become. For six weeks we have discovered the truth about identity. God gave each of us a special, powerful identity and in the giving of it, He has provided the tools we need to live in the fullness of our uniqueness and distinctiveness.

In Him we have value and worth and usefulness. In Him we have purpose and influence in the world we live in. He provides everything we need to flourish in our unique individuality. Yet we have also discovered that we have an enemy who wants to destroy us and steal our identity. An enemy who wants us to live less than we are and who desires for us to fail and falter and never reach our true potential. He will stop at nothing to derail our lives and push us out of our true identity into a false way of living.

We will battle the enemy throughout our lives because stealing our identity in Christ is the only tool he has available. Our strength comes from God who is constantly working in us and through us to make us more like Jesus.

> For we are God's handiwork, created in Christ Jesus to do good works, which God prepared in advance for us to do (Ephesians 2:10 NIV).

Even if your identity has been stolen or compromised, you can flourish, starting now. Turning from the enemy to Christ will help you recover the precious identity God intended for you all along. It may take some attitude adjustments and some decisions to be strong, but your love and hope will be revitalized in ways you can't imagine. Let's spend this last week together learning to flourish in our identity.

Week Seven
Day One
Potential

God created each of us with unique and exceptional characteristics. When we fully recognize our identity in the One who created us, we live in our greatest potential.

So who am I? I am a child of God. I belong to Him and He is my Father. My image is all wrapped up in Him. If I function in the strengths of my unique God-created personality and display His characteristics, others see me as being an illustration of Him. People identify Him with me and me with Him.

As we discovered in Week One, our true identity is rooted in God's image. When we grasp the reality of God's image in us, this truth will have a profound impact on how we view others and ourselves. We will begin to walk in our true identity, and our behavior will reflect Him. We are not God, but we show His image by taking on His values, attitudes, and character. The Holy Spirit equips us to live out our God-given identity. Without His wisdom and continued guidance from the Word, we will fall to every attack of our enemy.

Author Francis Frangipane wrote,

> "So many Christians are frozen in spiritual immaturity. They are easily offended, often distracted, and without prayer or spiritual discipline. We think God is requiring us simply to hang on, yet the Lord is looking for mature Christ-likeness to emerge within us. He feeds us with His Spirit and Word that we might have every resource we need to obtain His very life and character."[xxx]

None of us want to be "frozen in spiritual immaturity." We want mature Christ-likeness to emerge within us.

Read Proverbs 3:12:

> For whom the Lord loves He corrects, just as a father corrects the son in whom he delights (NKJV).

The Lord is our father and He loves us. According to this verse, what does He do because of this love?

_____
_____

When He corrects us, He demonstrates fatherly love for us. As our Father, He knows our image-bearing potential and He lovingly corrects us to bring out the fullness of that image.

Repeat the phrase "whom the Lord loves He corrects" aloud.

Many of us have experienced improper discipline from family members in childhood, and these inappropriate actions by people who were supposed to love us have distorted how we view God. His correction is full of love. God's way of correction will bring conviction not condemnation. He helps us see our failures and implants in us a desire to do right – not out of fear but out of love. God's correction is always specific, kind, and does not shame. The Lord's correction restores relationship.

One day I decided to return a new pair of shoes. I packed them into a shopping bag and made my way to the department store. I walked in, passed several clerks, and started browsing for a different pair.

About twenty minutes later, a salesperson approached me with a loud accusation, "Ma'am, you should have left your return in the front of the store." Her tone caught me off guard.

I responded, "I'll give them to the clerk at the desk after I pick out a new pair." She insisted that I take them to the front of the store immediately. Frustrated and agitated, I grew impatient, "Well, I was going to exchange these for another pair, but forget it. I don't want to own anything from this store!"

After a fifteen-minute drive home, I pulled into the garage and the Holy Spirit reminded me, "That's not who you are...."

My retaliation did nothing for me, except leave me shoeless and stressed. I knew an apology was in order. I called the store. Dialing was simple, but it wasn't necessarily easy. The result was so beneficial.

Yes, the clerk was rude and condescending, but my response was even worse because months before, during time in the Word and in prayer, I found a new understanding of my identity. I asked God to help me respond in kindness and humility to unfair situations. In the shoe store, I reacted with knee-jerk anger and responded with fury and retribution, but the Holy Spirit helped me calm down, see what I had done, and then behave according to my true identity by apologizing. The store manager accepted my apology, but my best reward was feeling the smile of God.

If we live in our full image-bearing potential, we will hear and obey God's correction.

Allow the Holy Spirit to affirm who you are according to the truth. Don't lower yourself to mediocrity or insignificance.

Wrong attitudes and inappropriate responses can cause us to bypass the truth if we aren't careful and diligent.

When we live in our full identity as a child of God, our attitudes change drastically. We have confidence and security. We are no longer complainers and self-serving. We will look for the best in people and be free from offense and grudges.

> However, as it is written: "What no eye has seen, what no ear has heard, and what no human mind has conceived"— the things God has prepared for those who love him (1 Corinthians 2:9 NIV).

According to the verse above, are there any limits placed on your potential if you love God? Explain.

_____
_____
_____
_____
_____

Most of us develop attitudes based on what is happening around us, the behavior of others, or our own performance. If the job is going well and the paycheck has a bonus or the scale shows a little weight loss and the new shoes are really cute, we go into the day with a bright, hopeful attitude. But if you don't feel well and your feet hurt and the car suddenly needs repair, or you feel impatient with your children and your boss yells at you, your attitude can take a dive.

God's attitude is one of grace and peace and hope. In our true identity, we are enabled by God to take on His attitudes even when our circumstances and feelings are all wrong. Living with a God-attitude is living in potential, but it is not going to occur unintentionally. It happens when we choose to recognize who we are in Christ Jesus and yield our lives to the power of the Holy Spirit within us.

Week Seven
Day Two
Supernatural

Living in true identity is not natural, it is supernatural. We are not expecting the bizarre or some magic, mystical existence, but God will intervene and guide us into beautiful places that might seem unearthly to those who don't know Him. He leads us to "still waters" (Psalm 23). He works for our good (Romans 8:28). He covers us with love.

As we focus on who we are in Christ, life will take on order and harmony, and a new rich character will develop. A person living in God's rhythms will not treat money, time, or relationships in ways that are dishonorable.

A person who bears the image of God lives with integrity and truth. If we keep His image in the forefront, we will not aim to cheat or cut corners. We identify with His character and live in an honorable way. We don't close our eyes to hurting people; we do our part for freedom, justice, anti-slavery, and fairness. We care for the poor, the under-privileged, and the sad and lonely ones who need love and a helping hand. He gifts us for these supernatural desires and abilities.

He also pours out other supernatural blessings on us.

Read Isaiah 40:29-31:

> He gives strength to the weary and increases the power of the weak. Even youths grow tired and weary, and young men stumble and fall; but those who hope in the LORD will renew their strength. They will soar on wings like eagles; they will run and not grow weary, they will walk and not be faint (NIV).

Read Matthew 7:7-8:

> Ask and it will be given to you; seek and you will find; knock and the door will be opened to you. For everyone who asks receives; the one who seeks finds; and to the one who knocks, the door will be opened (NIV).

What does God promise to do if we pray?

_____

If we ask, seek, and knock, He will answer. He is God and we have supernatural access to Him. If we believe our image is His image, we stop trying to become something we're not. Instead, we more fully realize and then become who we already are in Christ.

God made us and loves us. Our greatest successes and satisfaction come when we live in the identity He gave us.

Your future has great potential if you learn to wrap yourself in your true identity. We can clothe ourselves in the new identity and nature God has given us. Our goal is to be dressed in full knowledge, consistent with the image of the One who created us. Some of these characteristics are more supernatural than ordinary.

I want to wear mercy; I want to put on compassion; I want to walk in humility; I want to dress in peace. I want to adorn myself with unity and above all else, love unconditionally. These clothes fit my true identity. These are supernatural clothes.

You have a wealth of good things in you that come from your supernatural image in Christ. Read the following Scriptures and list the characteristics you possess.

Galatians 5:22–23:

> But the fruit of the Spirit is love, joy, peace, forbearance, kindness, goodness, faithfulness, gentleness and self-control. Against such things there is no law (NIV).

Proverbs 2:6:

> For the LORD gives wisdom; from his mouth come knowledge and understanding (NIV).

2 Timothy 2:7:

> Reflect on what I am saying, for the Lord will give you insight into all this (NIV).

1 John 4:13:

> This is how we know that we live in him and he in us: He has given us of his Spirit (NIV).

Romans 8:34:

> Who then is the one who condemns? No one. Christ Jesus who died—more than that, who was raised to life—is at the right hand of God and is also interceding for us (NIV).

_____
_____
_____
_____

As you look at these lists, notice the supernatural characteristics God has showered on you. You have love, joy, peace, patience, kindness, goodness, faithfulness, gentleness, and self-control. You have wisdom and knowledge. You have a sound mind. You have the Spirit of God living inside you. You have power. You have prayer. You have a prayer intercessor—Jesus—sitting at God's right hand. These are our God-given identity traits.

Read John 20:21-22:

> "As the Father has sent Me, I also send you." And when He had said this, He breathed on them, and said to them, "Receive the Holy Spirit" (NKJV).

According to these verses, what special power did the disciples receive in order to do the mission Jesus had for them to do?

_____
_____
_____

We are sent with authority by a leader who equips us for His calling. As Christ was in this world, so are we. And as Christ was sent to this world, so are we. You may believe you don't have what it takes, yet God has prepared you in Christ Jesus and enabled you with the power of His Spirit.

Jesus equips us for living within our true identity. He supernaturally endows us with the tools we need and the power of His Spirit so that we can live free of lies and illusions. We have a storehouse of great, amazing, unearthly abilities and skills. If we embrace the Word of God and listen to the Holy Spirit whisper, living in our true identity is a certainty.

Week Seven
Day Three
Love

I want to be free to love, free to serve, free to give. Not worried about who I am, but free to be all that I was created to be. In our God-given identity, we have great capacity to love. The love of Christ in us is far greater than any human love we could imagine.

According to 1 John 4:19, why do we have the capacity to love?

> We love because he first loved us (NIV).

_____
_____

When we live in our true identity, we begin to love the way He loved. When we receive His love, we then love. That's why it is critical to your identity to know the love of the Father.

During a recent Bible study, the speaker was introduced with these words: "She has an immense capacity to love." I pondered those words. It was true of this woman. The love of God filled her words.

I prayed, *God fill me up to the brim with love!*

Your identity is a love gift from God, and when you live fully in your identity, you will share the love with others. Have you noticed a central truth that is developing regarding our identity? When we understand and embrace our true identity, it will impact others.

Loving one another is not only an imitation of God's love to us, it is a big part of our identity in Him. He loves us ultimately and perfectly, and when we live in our God-given identity, our lives demonstrate love to others.

Loving others is also an outward expression of our inward love for God.

Paul spoke of this capacity to love in Romans 5:5:

> Such hope never disappoints or deludes or shames us, for God's love has been poured in our hearts through the Holy Spirit Who has been given to us (AMP).

How does this verse describe God's distribution of love?

_____
_____
_____

His love is not a little trickle. God's love is poured out. His love is distributed largely, spilled over, running over, and gushing out. Immense capacity.

When I flourish in my identity, I discover a new colossal ability to love others. Even those who aren't all that loveable.

> Loving one another is not only an imitation of God's love to us; it is also an outward expression of our inward love for God. In his first letter John refers to another commandment from God: 'This commandment we have from Him: that he who loves God must love his brother also' (1 John 4:21). If we claim to love the invisible God while we hate God's visible children, we are liars and hypocrites (1 John 4:20). Loving the children of God is the natural result of our love for their and our Father in heaven (1 John 5:1–2); we sometimes have to remind ourselves that other Christians are our brothers and sisters in Christ, members of the same family. If we love God, we will keep his commandments (1 John 5:3). John repeats this in 2 John 6 and ends up by coming back to where he started: God's commandment is that we should walk in love. If we love God, we will obey his commandments and, therefore, love one another.[xxxi]

As we consider how broad the love of God is in us, let's begin to think about people we know who need love. In the space below, write the names of a few people who need love. Ask God to help you find ways to love each one.

_____
_____

One afternoon I started a load of laundry and something happened to the washing machine. Water and suds poured over, gushed out onto the floor, down the hall, into the next room. I tried to turn the machine off, but it wouldn't stop. I'm not kidding. I couldn't get towels down fast enough to soak the water up. It's funny—now. I felt as if I was in one of those old *I Love Lucy* episodes. Romans 5:5 came to my mind. God fills us up with so much of His love and we just overflow.

His love is incredible. While it may seem too good to be true, His love is poured out into us to overflowing. If we believe anything else, we have believed a lie. First Corinthians 13, known as the love chapter, is an accurate and complete picture of our identity. Don't allow the familiarity of this passage to diminish its significance. Perhaps we have heard it so many times we just tune it out. The passage is a description of who we are in Christ Jesus.

Read 1 Corinthians 13:1-8 aloud.

> If I speak in the tongues of men or of angels, but do not have love, I am only a resounding gong or a clanging cymbal. If I have the gift of prophecy and can fathom all mysteries and all knowledge, and if I have a faith that can move mountains, but do not have love, I am nothing. If I give all I possess to the poor and give over my body to hardship that I may boast, but do not have love, I gain nothing. Love is patient. Love is kind. It does not envy, it does not boast, it is not proud. It does not dishonor others, it is not self-seeking, it is not easily angered, it keeps no record of wrongs. Love does not delight in evil but rejoices with the truth. It always protects, always trusts, always hopes, always perseveres. Love never fails (NIV).

What is the verb tense of this passage of Scripture?

_____

The tense is present tense. Love is a hear-and-now concept. Not "I will love you" or "I did love you," but "I love you now." The love of God is "now" love.

Read Romans 5:8:

> But God demonstrates his own love for us in this: While we were still sinners, Christ died for us.

Love. Demonstrate that love today. Whenever we behave any other way, we are not living according to our full image-bearing potential in Christ Jesus, nor do we love with the love He has poured into us.

As we live with Christ, our love grows more perfect and complete. He helps us love. Let's allow His love to keep growing. Get rid of the lies and deception of false identity. Be filled with love.

Week Seven
Day Four
Legacy

Duncan and I had a good friend who was a generous giver. He gave into others' life situations. He acted swiftly when he saw a need and did not wait for another opportunity or occasion. For him the time was always now. He has passed away and we miss him dearly, but I still think of him often because he left us something valuable. He left us a legacy. Not a legacy of money but a legacy of behavior. He demonstrated God's love. He loved generously. He was courteous and mindful of other people. He carried on meaningful conversations with the doorman at a hotel. He treated waiters in a restaurant with kindness. He'd say, "Let's just bless them today." Then he would leave a generous tip.

He freely opened up his home to others. He spoke kind and favorable words about his wife and told what a wonderful woman she was. He smiled constantly. If he went shopping for a pair of shoes for himself, he'd pick up an extra pair for a friend. He always had time to listen. He was an amazing encourager. If you saw your phone light up with his number, you wanted to answer. You knew he would communicate with enthusiasm and listen with grace. He taught us to do new things.

Unknowingly, he taught us how to bless others both physically and in words. Whenever you were around him, you felt love and you wanted to be in his presence. You felt safe. He was fun. He was trustworthy. His foundation was built on love – stable and unshakeable. He lived in his true identity. His life affected my life by helping me see my full potential.

Our friend was an exceptional man. His actions changed my perspective and activities. Do you have someone in your life – a friend, your mother, sister, teacher – who has made this kind of difference in your life? Who are those people in your life that have been a blessing to you? Who has demonstrated God's love to you? List them here and take a moment to thank God for their influence in your life.

_____
_____
_____

Look at the list again. Thank God that each person walks in his or her identity in Christ Jesus. Then pray for them. These people have left a legacy in your life.

A legacy is more than an inheritance of money or heirlooms. A legacy is life-changing and life-fulfilling. Living in your true identity will help you spread a legacy of love, joy, peace, and purpose into every situation you face.

God knows your full potential in Christ Jesus and He desires for you to know it. In fact, you have been given new life – a life not your own.

Read Galatians 2:20:

> I have been crucified with Christ and I no longer live, but Christ lives in me. The life I now live in the body, I live by faith in the Son of God, who loved me and gave himself for me (NIV).

Jesus gives us a way to connect with Him so that He will live in us and through us. He used the metaphor of the vine.

Read John 15:4-6:

> "Remain in me, as I also remain in you. No branch can bear fruit by itself; it must remain in the vine. Neither can you bear fruit unless you remain in me. "I am the vine; you are the branches. If you remain in me and I in you, you will bear much fruit; apart from me you can do nothing. If you do not remain in me, you are like a branch that is thrown away and withers; such branches are picked up, thrown into the fire and burned."

God does not see your rebellion, failures, or even your mistakes. He sees you as "in Christ." That means you have all the potential, all the power, and all the tools you need to leave a lasting legacy.

How would your attitude and choices change today if you saw yourself as God sees you?

_____
_____
_____

How would it affect your thoughts and actions toward others?

_____
_____
_____

God calls us to continue the work of Jesus in the world. God calls us to be soldiers, more than conquerors, deliverers, chosen ones, and disciples. We are to let the fragrance of His love and peace fill the space around us.

What have you done that continues the work of Jesus?

_____
_____
_____
_____
_____

Read John 14:6:

> Jesus said to him, "I am the way, the truth, and the life. No one comes to the Father except through me" (NKJV).

As we go through each day, the question is not always, "Is this right or wrong?" The real questions and decisions have to do with whether or not your actions bring life. "Does what I'm about to say or do show Christ's love and draw others to Him? If we allow Him, He will use our lips to spread His truth, our lives to show the way, and our hands to reach out in love.

Week Seven
Day Five
Reestablished

Remember the story of the Good Samaritan. A wounded man lay on the side of the road and several people passed by, and even though each one had the opportunity to assist the wounded man, they ignored him.

You have probably heard this story countless times and may even skim this paragraph believing you may know the outcome. This time, I ask you to slow down and read the account carefully.

Before you continue, pray, "Father, reveal something new in these words of Scripture."

Read Luke 10:30-37:

> A man was going down from Jerusalem to Jericho, and he fell among robbers, who stripped him and beat him and departed, leaving him half dead. Now by chance a priest was going down that road, and when he saw him he passed by on the other side. So likewise a Levite, when he came to the place and saw him, passed by on the other side. But a Samaritan, as he journeyed, came to where he was, and when he saw him, he had compassion. He went to him and bound up his wounds, pouring on oil and wine. Then he set him on his own animal and brought him to an inn and took care of him. And the next day he took out two denarii and gave them to the innkeeper, saying, 'Take care of him, and whatever more you spend, I will repay you when I come back.' Which of these three, do you think, proved to be a neighbor to the man who fell among the robbers?" He said, "The one who showed him mercy." And Jesus said to him, "You go, and do likewise" (ESV).

List the people mentioned in this parable.

_____
_____

What person in the story is like you and why?

_____

_____

_____

_____

When our identity has been stolen, we are like the wounded man. We have no hope or plans. No strategies or ideas. We have lost our identity. We can only be reestablished through the love and care of Jesus.

To be reestablished means the returning of something to its original state. Your identity was given to you by God when you accepted His gift of salvation. It is yours and yours alone. At that moment you had all the gifts and strengths and capacities you needed to fulfill His purpose in your life. But along the way the enemy stepped in the way with tricks and deceiving ideas and promises that weren't true, and he tried to steal your life. He wanted nothing more than to destroy you completely and keep you from your destiny. We've learned how crafty the enemy is and how successful he can be at identity theft, but we don't have to stay in the pit of despair because Jesus is ready and able to restore our soul and reestablish our life and destiny.

> He restores my soul; He leads me in the paths of righteousness for His name's sake (Psalm 23:3 NKJV).

The enemy may have attacked your health, but in the same way Jesus healed Peter's mother-in-law in, He will bring well-being and vigor back to you.

> Now He arose from the synagogue and entered Simon's house. But Simon's wife's mother was sick with a high fever, and they made request of Him concerning her. So He stood over her and rebuked the fever, and it left her. And immediately she arose and served them (Luke 4:38–39 NKJV).

The enemy may have blinded you about the truth of who you are in Christ, but Jesus opens blinded eyes just as He did for the man at the pool of Bethsaida.

> Then He put His hands on his eyes again and made him look up. And he was restored and saw everyone clearly (Mark 8:25 NKJV).

The enemy may have tried to silence your testimony with ruin and failure, but just as the man's tongue was loosened in Mark 7, ours will also be restored.

> Then they brought to Him one who was deaf and had an impediment in his speech, and they begged Him to put His hand on him. And He took him aside from the multitude, and put His fingers in his ears, and He spat and touched his tongue. Then, looking up to heaven, He sighed, and said to him, "Ephphatha," that is, "Be opened." Immediately his ears were opened, and the impediment of his tongue was loosed, and he spoke plainly (Mark 7:32–35 NKJV).

Perhaps the enemy has stolen financial resources and opportunities from you. He tried that trick long ago when he took every valuable from Job, but no devastation or storm or trial is too big for God to restore.

> And the LORD restored Job's losses when he prayed for his friends. Indeed the LORD gave Job twice as much as he had before (Job 42:10 NKJV).

> Now the LORD blessed the latter days of Job more than his beginning; for he had fourteen thousand sheep, six thousand camels, one thousand yoke of oxen, and one thousand female donkeys (Job 42:12 NKJV).

Identity lost can be reestablished by the power and love of God. I am determined to live in my true identity. You can too.

****
GOING DEEPER

Jesus told a parable about a woman who had lost a coin.

Read Luke 15:8-9:

> Or suppose a woman has ten silver coins and loses one. Doesn't she light a lamp, sweep the house and search carefully until she finds it? And when she finds it, she calls her friends and neighbors together and says, 'Rejoice with me; I have found my lost coin' (NIV).

How many coins did the woman have?

_____

From the story, can you determine how important the coin was to her?

_____

Once the coin was found, what did the woman do?

_____
_____
_____

The woman had ten silver drachma coins. These coins were each worth about one day's wages. Owning so few coins hints at her poverty. These ten coins may have been her dowry or the life savings of the family. When she discovered one of the coins was lost, she started a thorough search. She swept the house, lit a candle, and hunted carefully. She wouldn't quit. She swept and moved furniture until she found it.

One writer suggested it was as if you had a wedding band with ten diamonds around it. Then one day you discovered that one of the diamonds was missing. You wouldn't be satisfied with only having the nine that were left; you would search and search until you found the lost diamond.

So it is with your identity. Your identity has great value. If you lose any part of it, you are incomplete. If the enemy has stolen your God-given identity, begin now to sweep through your life to find it. Don't give up until you have discovered the truth of who you are in Christ Jesus.

Then just as the woman in the story celebrated with her friends over finding the coin, delight in your full true identity. The enemy is not invited to your party. Don't allow him to tattoo wrong thoughts on your mind.

In the appendix of this book, there is a list. Study these truths. Look up the Bible verses. As you study each verse, ask the Holy Spirit to reveal the truth of your identity and make it a reality in your heart and mind. Listen to any promptings of the Holy Spirit and be quick to adjust any mindsets or behaviors. God is at work in your life to conform and complete your identity. Breathe in Christ's promises. Believe in who God created you to be. He believes in you. Your identity is cause for great celebration. Rejoice.

> May the Lord make your love increase and overflow for each other and for everyone else, just as ours does for you. May he strengthen your hearts so that you will be blameless and holy in the presence of our God and Father when our Lord Jesus comes with all his holy ones (1 Thessalonians 3:12–13 NIV).

.

Appendix
POWERFUL TRUE-IDENTITY DECLARATIONS

The more you agree with God about your identity in Christ, the more your life will reflect Him. The more fully you live in your true identity, the less opportunities the enemy will have to steal your identity from you.

Learn to see yourself as God sees you. Accept what God says about you and become the spiritual person you are.

Understanding who you are in Christ will give you a strong foundation to build your life on. Knowing who you are in Jesus is the key to a successful Christian life.

Your identity doesn't depend on something you do or have done. Your true identity is who you are in Christ. When you are in Christ, you are a new creation, the old has passed away.

If my identity has been stolen:	**In my God-given identity:**
I might as well be dead.	I am alive in Christ. Ephesians 2:5
No one loves me.	I am loved. 1 John 3:3
No one likes me.	I am accepted. Ephesians 1:6
I am an orphan.	I am a child of God. John 1:12
I am friendless.	I am Jesus' friend. John 15:14
I am poor.	I am a joint heir with Jesus. Romans 8:17
I am alone.	I am united with God and one spirit with Him. 1 Corinthians 6:17
God doesn't care about me.	I am a temple of God. He lives in me. 1 Corinthians 6:19

If my identity has been stolen:	In my God-given identity:
I don't belong.	I am a member of Christ's body. 1 Corinthians 12:27
I have no legacy.	I am a saint. Ephesians 1:1
I have failed.	I am redeemed and forgiven. Colossians 1:14
I need more.	I am complete in Jesus Christ. Colossians 2:10
I am a captive.	I am free from condemnation. Romans 8:1
I'll never change.	I am a new creation because I am in Christ. 2 Corinthians 5:17
I have no purpose.	I am established, anointed, and sealed by God. 2 Corinthians 1:21
I am afraid.	I do not have a spirit of fear, but of love, power, and a sound mind. 2 Timothy 1:7; Isaiah 54:14
I have no help or direction.	I am God's co-worker. 2 Corinthians 6:1; Philippians 2:13
I wallow in sin.	I am seated in heavenly places with Christ. Ephesians 2:6
God doesn't hear me.	I have direct access to God. Ephesians 2:18
I am useless.	I am one of God's living stones. 1 Peter 2:5
God is missing.	I can always know the presence of God because He never leaves me. Hebrews 13:5

If my identity has been stolen:	**In my God-given identity:**
I can't do it.	All things through Him are possible. Luke 18:27
I'm tired.	He gives me rest. Matthew 11:28-30
I can't go forward.	I can continue because He gives grace. 2 Corinthians 12:9
I don't know which way to go.	He directs my paths. Proverbs 3:5-6
I don't have enough.	He supplies all I need. Philippians 4:19
My burdens are too heavy.	When I'm worried and frustrated, I cast all my cares on Him. 1 Peter 5:7
I am captive.	I am free from the law of sin and death. Romans 8:2
The enemy will hurt me.	I am born of God; the evil one does not touch me. 1 John 5:18.
I am ignorant.	I have the mind of Christ. 1 Corinthians 3:16; Philippians 2:5
I am anxious.	I have the peace of God that passes all understanding. Philippians 4:7
I cannot serve God.	I am a doer of the Word and blessed in my actions. James 1:22, 25
I am defeated.	I am more than a conqueror through Him who loves me. Romans 8:37
Darkness covers me.	I am the light of the world. Matthew 5:14

If my identity has been stolen:	**In my God-given identity:**
I have nothing to say for Him.	I am called of God to be the voice of His praise. Psalm 66:8; 2 Timothy 1:9
I am ill.	I am healed by the stripes of Jesus. Isaiah 53:5; 1 Peter 2:24
I am weak.	I am strengthened with all might according to His power. Colossians 1:11

 **Laurie Dodds** has a heart for women. Her teaching inspires women of all ages and backgrounds to experience the reality of God's presence and helps them build a strong self-image, growing into godly women, supportive wives, and loving mothers.

Whether she is leading a small group or women's Bible study, ministering at women's prisons, teaching at a women's conference or a church service, Laurie has the passion and commitment to help women fall in love with God and accomplish His unique purpose and plan for their lives.

Since receiving her degree from Vanderbilt University, Laurie has served with numerous churches including Second Baptist with Pastor Ed Young and Lakewood Church with Pastor Joel Osteen. Laurie is an author, teacher, speaker, and has written articles and blogs for numerous ministries around the world.

Laurie and her husband, Duncan, have three grown daughters and live in Texas.

Other books by Laurie Dodds:

Regret, Rehearse, Rejoice
Identity Theft

Contact Laurie for your next event.

Email: dodds.laurie@gmail.com
Website: www.lauriedodds.com
Website: www.ibelieveispeak.com

Follow Laurie on

 Laurie Dodds

@lauriedodds

[i] Psalm 139:14 (NIV) I praise you because I am fearfully and wonderfully made; your works are wonderful, I know that full well.

[ii] Brian Houston Hillsong Church Podcast "Identity! Just How Do You See Yourself?"

[iii] Robert S. McGee, *The Search for Significance* (Nashville, Tennessee, Thomas Nelson, Revised edition (July 17, 2003) 20

[iv] Ibid, page 21

[v] Adapted from Walvoord, J. F., Zuck, R. B., & Dallas Theological Seminary. (1985). *The Bible Knowledge Commentary: An Exposition of the Scriptures* (Ps 139:13–18). Wheaton, IL: Victor Books.

[vi] Dockery, D. S., Butler, T. C., Church, C. L., Scott, L. L., Ellis Smith, M. A., White, J. E., & Holman Bible Publishers (Nashville, T. (1992). *Holman Bible Handbook* (134–135). Nashville, TN: Holman Bible Publishers.

[vii] Adapted from Voices of the True Woman movement Nancy Leigh DeMoss Copyright 2010 Moody Publishers page 38-39

[ix] *Deepening Your Ministry Through Prayer and Personal Growth: 30 Strategies to Transform Your Ministry.* 1996 (M. Shelley, Ed.) (1st ed.). Library of Christian leadership (143). Nashville, TN: Moorings.

[x] Author's notes taken from a presentation by Will Walker – Providence Church (Podcast 1-1-2012) "The Gospel & New Year's Resolutions"

[xi] C.S. Lewis, "First and Second Things," in *God in the Dock: Essays on Theology and Ethics* (Eerdmans, 1994), p. 280.

[xii] This is from The Gifts of Imperfection by Brene Brown 2010 Hazelden Center City Minnesota page 24

[xiii] Daily Hope with Rick Warren Friday April 15, 2011 Devotional from Purpose Driven Connection

[xiv] James 4:8 (NIV) Come near to God and he will come near to you. Wash your hands, you sinners, and purify your hearts, you double-minded.

[xv] Barnes Commentary

[xvi] Used with permission Marsha Baumgartner

[xvii] Laura Kates – Bible teacher and mentor

[xviii] Kesler, J. (1988). *Vol. 13: Being holy, being human: Dealing with the expectations of ministry.* The Leadership Library (180–181). Carol Stream, IL; Waco, TX: Christianity Today, Inc.; Word Books.

[xix] Mark Batterson, 2011, *The Circle Maker*, Michigan: Zondervan. pg 76

[xx] Renee Garner, April 11, 2012

[xxi] Christine Cain – twitter

[xxii] Used with permission Chase Jaffarian

[xxiii] Hardman, S. G., & Moody, D. L. (1997). *Thoughts for the quiet hour.* Willow Grove, PA: Woodlawn Electronic Publishing.

[xxiv] Warren, Rick (2002). *The Purpose Driven Life.* Michigan: Zondervan.pg 11-12

[xxv] Chuck Swindoll, *Insight for Today-Daily Devotional,* March 12, 2012

[xxvi] Francis Frangipayne

[xxvii] Timothy Keller, *The Prodigal God* (New York, New York, Penguin, Riverhead Trade, 2011) 114

[xxviii] Quote from Shirley Kelly

[xxix] Adapted from Prime, D. (2005). *Opening up 1 Corinthians.* Opening Up Commentary (92–94). Leominister: Day One Publications.

[xxx] Francis F. notation needed

[xxxi] Crosby, T. P. (2006). *Opening up 2 and 3 John.* Opening Up Commentary (32–33). Leominster: Day One Publications.

Made in the USA
Charleston, SC
21 March 2013